Honey, I
Shrunk the devil!

How to Recognize and Minimize Your Enemy

By Dianne Sloan

Treasure House

An Imprint of
Destiny Image® Publishers, Inc.
P.O. Box 310
Shippensburg, PA 17257-0310

"For where your treasure is,
there will your heart be also." Matthew 6:21

ISBN 0-7684-3026-7

For Worldwide Distribution
Printed in the U.S.A.

First Printing: 2000   Second Printing: 2000

This book and all other Destiny Image, Revival Press, MercyPlace, Fresh Bread, and Treasure House books are available at Christian bookstores and distributors worldwide.

For a U.S. bookstore nearest you, call **1-800-722-6774**.
For more information on foreign distributors,
call **717-532-3040**.
Or reach us on the Internet: **http://www.reapernet.com**.

Dedication

I would like to dedicate this book to my mother, Maurine Essary, whose humor and wit left an indelible print upon my personality. She has painted the family with bright colors and cast the dye by her unique pattern of thinking.

To my father, Harold Essary, who taught me impeccable character and principles, I will be forever indebted.

Also, to my grandsons whom I trust will be fourth generation "devil shrinkers"—Chandler, Jordan, and Andrew—I give these truths to know your heritage in Christ and never shirk from destroying evil.

To the many around the world whose hearts seek after God, to know Him and fear only Him, I dedicate these pages.

Last but not least, to those who walk beside me in ministry, I respect you, love you, and appreciate you in ways too numerous to list. Thanks for tolerating my humorous but direct approach to life when you are trying to appeal to deep reasoning.

Acknowledgments

I would like to acknowledge Johnny, my husband of more than 30 years, for his unselfish contribution to this project and to me. His knowledge of Scripture and his organizational skills were invaluable.

In addition, to the people whose stories I shared, I thank you for allowing God to speak to me through you. Each of you has contributed a lesson that will never be forgotten.

Endorsements

This is what one preacher's kid/preacher's wife has to say about another preacher's kid/preacher's wife. Dianne Sloan is a deeply sensitive, spiritually discerning, compassionate nurturer. She is an extremely loyal lady who has the ability to tell you what she thinks without making you mad. She can do this because you know that she has in mind what is best for you. Even though she is marvelously used of God, she is neither boastful nor condescending. Diane is fun to be around, and this book is just a glimpse of her wholehearted life.

GayNell and Cleddie Keith
Heritage Fellowship
Florence, Kentucky

I have had the privilege of ministering and traveling with Dianne often; she has been a source of inspiration and a lot of good laughs. Her book reflects her transparency and honesty, and is peppered with wisdom learned the hard way. Her sharp insight has been a wonderful point of reference for me. Seeing my near exhaustion in ministry, she has spoken into my life and given me godly counsel. I count her a valuable friend and encourage you to keep a copy of *Honey, I Shrunk the devil!* close at hand, to read again and again.

Lila Terhune
Brownsville Assembly of God
Pensacola, Florida

Dianne Sloan is an unforgettable human being whose heart and passion for the Body of Christ worldwide overflows from the moment you meet her. She has already touched the nations with her keen prophetic understanding, her heart of compassion, and her rich ministry in the Word. This latest work from her pen is sure to do the same. Hers indeed is a "ministry of deliverance" and with her buoyant spirit and unique way of communication, she invites us to realize how to minimize our opponent so that he cannot get the best of us. Dianne's contribution to the subject of spiritual warfare is sure to provide necessary food, stamina, encouragement, hope and a big smile for all who are willing to believe the truth, receive it, and act on it. The insights in the volume you now hold flow like a river of refreshing that is sure to water your thirsting soul.

Dr. Mark J. Chironna
Master's Touch International Church

Dianne is taking the treasures she has gleaned in this field—from having been a preacher herself, a pastor's wife, and a very successful minister among the nations—and she is putting them in book form so that many others can benefit from them. Dianne Sloan is a winner, and she wants to teach you how to be a winner too—spiritually, physically, emotionally, and in every other area of life. Through the message of this book, everything that has been a detriment in your life will become a stepping-stone to victory. Dianne Sloan's life experience will open avenues of victory in which you have never yet walked. I encourage you to read this book and be changed

Ruth Ward Heflin
Ashland, Virginia

It is my priviledge to highly recommend Dianne Sloan's book, *Honey, I Shrunk the devil!* Upon reading this book, words like revelatory, insightful, unique, creative, and inspiring ran through my mind. Dianne shares out of years of experience walking with the Lord through the good, bad, and the humdrum. Through it all she has been given some very strategic Holy Spirit tools as to how to expose both the identity and tactics of the enemy. Tested and tried in the "trenches of everyday life," Dianne has also learned the "Way of Victory." You will laugh, cry, and shout as you read through Dianne's creative and humorous approach to a most serious subject. I regard it as a rich honor to count Dianne Sloan as one of my dear friends and co-laborers in times such as these as together we learn even more effectively to "shrink the devil" and exalt our Lord Jesus!

Dotty Schmitt
Immanuel's Church
Silver Spring, Maryland

Dianne Sloan is real and her humor and wit are refreshing. I know her to be a God chaser. Her love and devotion for God will inspire you. She's a graduate of the "school of hard knocks" and we all can learn from her experiences.

Brenda Kilpatrick
Brownsville Assembly of God
Pensacola, Florida

Contents

Preface

The goals of any speaker should be to say things to which people can relate and to say them in a way that can be remembered. When the Lord first put the message, "Honey, I Shrunk the devil," into my spirit, I never dreamed I would be asked to adapt it for publication. My deep desire now is no different than it was then. I want to do three things in this writing:

1. Exalt the Lord

2. Expose the devil

3. Explain how you can win

In these pages I have attempted to be transparent and tell you about my own journey. It is my sincere prayer that you will be inspired to rise up to conquer any and every foe in your life. Most of these foes are within, so you can expect the victory to be where the battle rages. *Honey, I Shrunk the Devil* is intended to help you have a winning strategy for life. Victory is yours for the taking. You are more than a conqueror, but maximizing your potential and minimizing your enemy is not automatic.

HONEY, I SHRUNK THE DEVIL!

You will have to execute a plan for shrinking the devil, whose over-inflated image often hides the face of God! Deflate and defeat satan and stand in awe of our magnificent Lord!

Introduction

Devil shrinking has long been an interest of mine. Since childhood I have had a strong sense of God's presence. I gave my heart to Christ at the tender age of four in a small, wood-framed church in western Kentucky. The thing I remember most about that place is that it was located on the front lot of a cemetery. This cemetery was my playground and place of worship. Undisturbed, except for the occasional funeral procession, I went about to inform those already departed of their impending doom. The rows of tombstones stood respectfully and pierced the sky like a great sea of people to hear me preach my first messages. I already knew at the age of four that I would proclaim the gospel of Jesus Christ, and I remained preoccupied with spiritual things throughout all of my adolescent life. As long as I can remember I always wanted to be a preacher.

My older sister and I were often heard singing, preaching, and dancing in the yards as we reenacted the mannerisms of the old saints. When we children would "play church," I always wanted to be the preacher. One day my grandmother heard me arguing with my sister about who was going to preach. I finally won the prized spot and we began the service with exuberant singing. After "I'll Fly Away" and a few other well-known songs, the time came for the introduction of the preacher. My sister stood and made the announcement, "Now we want to ask 'Sister Essary' (my maiden name) to come preach." I arose and stood behind the make-believe pulpit (this time a stump) only to exclaim, "I cannot preach today because the devil has got me!"

My precious Baptist grandma, Vina Walker, overheard us and concluded that I had heard my preacher dad make that statement. She would later laughingly relate this story about our favorite pastime many times. It seemed my early perception was that satan was stronger than believers and could hold them back at his will. I had no doubt discerned in my young spirit that church people were paralyzed by fear and doubt. They were often unable to do what they were supposed to do because "the devil had them." After all, I had seen many people refuse to participate in the meetings, giving one excuse or another. I had concluded it was the result of being bound by the devil. So you see my interest in devil shrinking was an early preoccupation that remains to this day.

Today I am still appalled that many people in the Church live as though the power of God is limited. At the same time they over-magnify the image of satan. Have we an incapacitated God and an all-powerful big devil? Too many people have a serious distortion in their view of spiritual things. It seems as though they are peering through the wrong end of the telescope, causing God to become small while magnifying satan's might. Sometimes we hear religious people speak about demonic activity as though it were some overpowering force, and speak of God as though He is on public assistance and badly disabled. The "big devil" Bible verse that is often quoted is: "…your adversary the devil, as a roaring lion, walketh about, seeking whom he may devour" (1 Pet. 5:8).

Speaking of our world, people say, "It's a jungle out there." Satan is then viewed as the king of this jungle. It is often thought that we are left to his whims and that he devours whom he chooses, when he chooses, and where he chooses. After all, doesn't the Bible say something like that? No, the Scripture says he seeks whom he "may" devour. He looks for people who will let him win. Too many Christians "shrink" away in the presence of the demon spirits that come against them. Instead, they need to rise up and shrink the devil standing in front of them. We must set the record straight. We are not doomed to be subject to the wiles and wishes of satan. He is not greater than our God. No way! We serve a great big Almighty God, and we have a very limited foe. A popular praise song by Bob Crutchley contains the line, "Great big God, little bitty devil." Satan's limits are not set by us, but rather by God. It is apparent to me that when we fear God, we need not fear man or the devil. But if we do not fear God, we will be left to fear both man and satan. Maybe fearing the wrong person is the real problem after all. When fear is misplaced, perspective is lost. Jesus said, "And fear not them which kill the body, but are not able to kill the soul: but rather fear him which is able to destroy both soul and body in hell" (Mt. 10:28).

Since preaching the message, "Honey, I Shrunk the devil," I have had numerous people approach me to say they were enlightened and blessed by learning how to shrink the devils that have come against them. Changing our perspective to God's perspective allows us to shift into a new paradigm. In reality, God is all-powerful while satan operates within sovereign limitations. Followers of Jesus Christ would be quick to say they agree, yet often their lives contradict this basic fact.

Honey, I Shrunk the devil!

We fear the devil and even fall prey to his elementary tactics. This book will help you look through the right end of the telescope. God will become larger and satan will become smaller in your perspective. You can actually shrink the impact of the devil and minimize his damage to you and your family.

I like to run through the corridors of Scripture and gather truths that tell me what is necessary to live an overcoming life. I am interested in the spiritual principles that apply "where the rubber meets the road." Among the many vital things I discovered in the Word are two very basic, but very important truths—knowing who I am in God and, knowing who God is in me. When I know and understand these two things, I realize satan is not really "in the loop." The devil only gets into the game if someone lets him join in the play. The Word of God teaches us we are "...hid with Christ in God" (Col. 3:3b). Like Paul, we can testify, "...I live; yet not I, but Christ liveth in me..." (Gal. 2:20). Jesus Christ has already fought the battle at Calvary. When He won we were in Him and He was in us. Just as when David killed Goliath and won the battle for every Israelite, the victory Christ won is our victory (see 1 Sam. 17). Sometimes I want to jump up and shout, "We won! We won!"

While I was growing up, my family developed many meaningful relationships with other ministry families. One of these dear families was the A.W. Harrison family from Oklahoma City, Oklahoma. Chief Harrison, as he was affectionately called, was a Native American brother with a sizeable family. My father was conducting revival services at his church when Chief told us the following "grandpa" story.

Chief was preaching at his church while his four-year-old grandson was playing on the second pew. In his message, Chief was building a battleground between David and Goliath. Little did he realize the young boy was actually listening to the sermon. After all, he seemed to be quite preoccupied with his toys. Chief dramatically presented the Old Testament classic.

Goliath was in the valley calling out threats and mocking God's army. He was defying the God of Israel. The nine-foot giant's voice shook the ground as he boomed out his challenge: "Who will fight? Who will be the final champion?" As the preacher told the story, the church was very quiet while suspense mounted. Suddenly from the second pew came a voice, "Kill him, Grandad, kill him!" Needless to say, that broke the silence.

Friend, the devil is a foe already defeated. When we submit ourselves to God and resist the devil, we have the power to overcome the enemy and diminish his effect upon our lives (see Jas. 4:7). Even the weakest saint with pure faith in Christ has the power to overcome satan. Overcoming is accomplished by not yielding to the devil, believing his deceptions, succumbing to his schemes, or falling into his traps. We must recognize him and rise up to resist him, exercising our authority through Jesus Christ. When we resist the devil he flees, which means he runs like a flea. Instead of some mighty overpowering force, he becomes a fleeing flea. From a roaring lion to a running flea? Wow! We just shrunk the devil. The more we submit to God and the more we resist the devil, the bigger our God gets and the smaller the devil becomes in our lives.

Isn't it time you shrunk your devil down to size and won your personal victory? Get ready to join me on a journey to victory that ends with a victory dance known as "The Devil Stomp." I will guide you on this journey and point out the scenery, because I have already made such a journey in my personal life and ministry. I've watched the devils that have come against me shrink before my eyes. I've shrunk devils of burnout, depression, poverty, and apathy, just to name a few. I've learned how satan gains entrance and how to show him to the exit.

In writing this book, it is my sincere desire and prayer that my practical and insightful approach to life will bring you into greater personal freedom and spiritual fullness. You, too, can be a devil shrinker!

> *Now unto him that is able to keep you from falling, and to present you faultless before the presence of His glory with exceeding joy, to the only wise God our Saviour, be glory and majesty, dominion and power, both now and forever. Amen* (Jude 24-25).

Chapter One

Devil Shrinking 101

The Classroom of the Spirit

Come with me now into the classroom of the Holy Spirit. The course of study includes a "workbook," a "laboratory" for experiments and yes, there will be a test! But do not make this a "crash course." Rather, take your time and learn how to rise above any and every opposing circumstance in your life. There will be difficult times of testing. You will be tried and proven, but there is genuine hope for your success. Many students before you have graduated from this course with flying colors. One of the early graduates wrote:

> *For I am now ready to be offered, and the time of my departure is at hand. I have fought a good fight, I have finished my course, I have kept the faith: Henceforth there is laid up for me a crown of righteousness, which the Lord, the righteous judge, shall give me at that day: and not to me only, but unto all them also that love His appearing* (2 Timothy 4:6-8).

There will also be a diploma given upon the successful completion of your course of study. Each student will receive a

1

plaque of recognition with the engraved words, "Well done, good and faithful servant" (Mt. 25:23). And the person handing out the diplomas and recognition will be the Creator of the universe, the King of kings and the Victor over death, hell, and the grave. He has been given all power in Heaven and earth. He is the man who carries the keys to hell. That's right, contrary to what some people believe, the devil does not even have the keys to his own house!

This little study guide, *Honey, I Shrunk the devil*, and the official textbook, the Holy Bible, can assist and equip you in completing your course of study. Other students in the class may discuss ideas and encourage you, but you will have to do your own work. To complete this class successfully you will need to work out your own deliverance. As a teacher's assistant, my goal for each student is simply "...that they may recover themselves out of the snare of the devil, who are taken captive by him at his will" (2 Tim. 2:26).

Before we begin our coursework, let's note that there are two primary facts about the world in which we live—there is a God and there is a devil. There is also one primary question each person will at some point answer: Who is bigger?

While there is no question who is actually greater in the universe and who will ultimately reign supreme, human perception varies from person to person. This perception determines to what degree a person will conquer and overcome his or her enemies. Some people see the devil as being too big for God to handle, let alone someone they themselves can conquer. For those who see or fear the "big monster," I offer a practical plan to shrink the devil. Together we can make him small enough to stomp! For those who have already discovered how to minimize the enemy, these pages will help to keep him small and not allow him to grow in their lives! Now, let's get down to business with some basic principles.

Each of us faces our own demons in life. Devils come in all shapes and sizes. The size of devil dispatched to oppose some- one is generally directly related to his or her level of spiritual development and importance in the Kingdom of God. In other words, someone may be fighting a little devil, but because of his early or limited spiritual impact, he could be struggling as much as another person dealing with stronger demons. This is most likely because the second person's life is on a much high- er spiritual plane. Additionally, the type of service or ministry a person provides to society may attract more or bigger devils. This is why we are taught by the apostle Paul to pray for "kings and all who are in authority..." (see 1 Tim. 2:2). Not everyone is fighting the same size of devil, yet God gives grace and power for every hour. Sometimes the small cross is actually heavier because of the material from which it is made. Satan sees to it that no one glides through his Christian journey.

As a young teenager, I remember sharing with my mother about my call into the ministry. I will never forget her counsel. She said, "Dianne, you have to know you are called to ministry or you will not survive. You won't ever meet the devil until you start preaching." My 14-year-old mind could not comprehend that concept. However, nearly 30 years down the road when I suffered from ministry burnout, I understood all too well what she meant that day. It is true that when you move into a new dimension of service or reach a higher plateau, you may well find you are confronted with higher-ranking demon powers. The cliché we use today is "a new level, a new devil."

The techniques and truths presented in this book have been tried, tested, and proven during the 40 years since I began preaching as a teenage girl. I have faced many battles in the physical, spiritual, and emotional realms of life. I have met the devil and been wounded in battle. Yet, I am winning the war as

3

the nature of Christ continues to increase within me and the power of the enemy diminishes around me. I am an "overcomer." And you will be, too, after you learn the art of devil shrinking.

Regardless of the size and shape of your enemy, the goal is to shrink him down to a point where you can consistently, victoriously overcome! Satan is shrinkable! No matter what the circumstance is, if you take proper action your testimony can be, "Honey, I shrunk the devil." Rest assured that God wants you to win this war! His Word declares: "Ye are of God, little children, and have overcome them: because greater is He that is in you, than he that is in the world" (1 Jn. 4:4).

Jesus Christ conquered the devil at Calvary, as seen in His resurrection power, and his victory is your victory. As the Word declares, "Thanks be to God, which giveth us the victory through our Lord Jesus Christ" (1 Cor. 15:57).

Our primary requirement for devil shrinking must be to have solid footing in the Word of God. We must know and understand what the Bible says about our enemy. From the Holy Scriptures we know that God is greater than the devil. We are assured the power of Christ makes us "...more than conquerors..." (Rom. 8:37). Satan may knock you down, but he can't knock you out if you have Jesus in your heart. The apostle Paul wrote to the Romans and assured them that nothing, absolutely nothing could cause them to lose. Likewise for us, nothing other than our own choice to reject the love and power of Jesus can leave us without hope of victory over the enemy. Consider the apostle's words:

> *Who shall separate us from the love of Christ? Shall tribulation, or distress, or persecution, or famine, or nakedness, or peril, or sword? As it is written, For Thy sake we are killed all the day long; we are accounted as sheep for the slaughter. Nay, in all these things we are*

more than conquerors through him that loved us. For I am persuaded, that neither death, nor life, nor angels, nor principalities, nor powers, nor things present, nor things to come, nor height, nor depth, nor any other creature, shall be able to separate us from the love of God, which is in Christ Jesus our Lord (Romans 8:35-39).

As we continue to study devil shrinking, let us answer the question, "Who is the devil?" All great military experts will attest to the fact that you must learn all you can about your opponent.

The Truth About the Liar

The devil is indeed a spirit being and is exposed and explained in the Holy Scriptures in the following seven ways:

1.   Originally, the devil was an angel named lucifer created by God. Lucifer rebelled against the authority of God, choosing to rule hell rather than serve Heaven.

2.   When lucifer, who became known as satan, rebelled, one third of the angels followed him. This means God has two holy angels for every unholy devil. (Note: I could have written a book twice this size on angels.)

3.   Satan has an inherent resentment and hatred for the human race because of God's plan and intention for us to dominate the earth.

4.   Satan is diametrically opposed to and constantly at war with God. He uses human beings as the "pawns" on the chess board in an ongoing competition with the King.

5. Satan is limited in his scope of power. God created us with the power of choice and our use of that power enables or disables satan's power in our lives.

6. Jesus Christ has conquered satan. His victory is our victory through faith. We have been given power over the enemy. We are more than conquerors!

7. God alone will reign supreme in the universe. In the end, satan will be in a lake of fire forever and those who have overcome him will rule and reign with Christ in the new Heaven and the new earth. This will be a world without sin or satan.

Genesis, the book of beginnings, introduces satan as a divested angel who is trying to regain his position and status on earth. Most Bible scholars believe he was cast out of Heaven and relinquished a previously held dominion on earth to man, God's crowning creation. It is no wonder, then, that satan made his initial approach to those to whom God had given earthly dominion. To regain his rulership of planet earth, satan tricked, tempted, and trapped humans into surrendering to his intentions. Satan is a thief and a liar. His nature, motives, and strategies have not changed since he was in the garden of Eden. Appearing often as an angel of light, one of his many disguises, his goals are anything but angelic. They are demonic. He is out to hurt you and everyone you love. Yes, someone is out to get you and that someone is the devil. "The thief cometh not, but for to steal, and to kill, and to destroy: I am come that they might have life, and that they might have it more abundantly" (Jn. 10:10).

If people on earth would fully resist and not yield to the wiles of the devil, his power would be gone (see Eph. 6:11). We have the authority and he seeks to cause us to forfeit our God-given rights. To advance God's Kingdom and stop the devil in his tracks, we must know how he operates and locate his limitations. They are many! Yet none of them are new. Satan is using the same tactics he used in the garden of Eden with Adam and Eve.

> *Now the serpent was more subtle than any beast of the field which the Lord God had made. And he said to the woman, Yea, hath God said, Ye shall not eat of every tree of the garden? And the woman said unto the serpent, We may eat of the fruit of the trees of the garden: but of the fruit of the tree which is in the midst of the garden, God hath said, Ye shall not eat of it, neither shall ye touch it, lest ye die. And the serpent said unto the woman, Ye shall not surely die: For God doth know that in the day ye eat thereof, then your eyes shall be opened, and ye shall be as gods, knowing good and evil. And when the woman saw that the tree was good for food, and that it was pleasant to the eyes, and a tree to be desired to make one wise, she took the fruit thereof, and did eat, and gave also unto her husband with her; and he did eat. And the eyes of them both were opened, and they knew that they were naked; and they sewed fig leaves together and made themselves aprons. And they heard the voice of the Lord God walking in the garden in the cool of the day: and Adam and his wife hid themselves from the presence of the Lord God amongst the trees of the garden (Genesis 3:1-8).*

After doubt began to work, Eve added some human reasoning. Next satan actually contradicted what God had said. He lied to our human parents in the beginning and he is still lying today. If satan really had something to offer those made of clay, why did he not propose it in the beginning? If he is worth following and serving in his kingdom, should he not rightfully produce something that he himself owns? The truth is, he can't. He has nothing! He is broke! Bankrupt! He has no tangible property! He is an outcast and is trying to regain control through deception. When will we stop buying into his schemes and believing his outrageous lies? Whenever anyone chooses to say "no" to his wicked plans and to cease tolerating his torment, the devil shrinks in his or her presence. The real power for overcoming is to love and follow the truth of God, as revealed in His Word, His Son, and the Holy Spirit. Those who do not stand for the truth always fall for the lie.

> *Even him, whose coming is after the working of satan with all power and signs and lying wonders, and with all deceivableness of unrighteousness in them that perish; because they received not the love of the truth, that they might be saved. And for this cause God shall send them strong delusion, that they should believe a lie: that they all might be damned who believed not the truth, but had pleasure in unrighteousness* (2 Thessalonians 2:9-12).

In the wilderness temptation, Jesus Christ met and was challenged by the devil. This was the real devil, the former angel himself, lucifer. It is doubtful that anyone else, other than Adam and Eve, has really dealt with the devil himself. We make general references to satan or the devil, but in actuality we are dealing with unclean spirits or fallen angels. These beings make up the host of demons operating in the kingdom of darkness. However, for the sake of simplicity and understanding, we will refer to the "whatevers" or "whoevers" that bring an attack upon your life as being the devil. The devil indeed, but one that is shrinkable!

Now that we understand who we are talking about when we refer to the devil, let's move on to some practical methods for devil shrinking.

Will Shrink in Hot Water

A vital key to devil shrinking is that it must be done in hot water. Warm or lukewarm water won't do. His stronghold increases in lukewarm Christian lives or cold, unbelieving hearts. The church at Laodicea was lulled into lukewarm living. In the last of the seven letters of Revelation to the seven churches, our Lord admonished Laodicea, saying:

I know thy works, that thou art neither cold nor hot: I would thou wert cold or hot. So then because thou art lukewarm, and neither cold nor hot, I will spue thee out of my mouth (Revelation 3:15-16).

Those who are cold usually know it. Being cold is better than the self-deception in which Laodicea lived. This is why God would rather have someone cold than lukewarm. Of course, the real goal is to be hot for God! Being lukewarm means a person has spiritual apathy, which allows our enemy to gain a foothold and rise up against us.

We must be a passionate people to overcome the power of the devil. Several years ago, the Holy Spirit prompted me to starve my fears and feed my passion for God. As my spiritual passion increased, the devil seemingly decreased in size. I will share some of the details of how God taught me to starve my fears and feed my passion for Him in a later chapter.

In the first letter to the seven churches (see Rev. 2:1-10), Jesus rebuked the church at Ephesus for losing its first love. First love is passionate love, and He commanded them to repent or risk being removed. Christ will not tolerate a cold-hearted lover. He will not play second fiddle. He is first chair or none at all.

What is the problem with a lukewarm Christian? Lukewarm water is the result of compromise, of mixing the hot and the cold. Too many Christians have mingled the things of God with the things of the world, leaving them lukewarm. Keeping spiritual passion hot requires separating from the coldness of the world. Sin is the culprit that gives people a cold heart. Jesus said, "And because iniquity shall abound, the love of many shall wax cold" (Mt. 24:12). We must get sin out of our lives. Sin dilutes our spiritual passion and lowers the temperature of our fervor and zeal for God. The end result is lukewarm religion, which is not a deterrent for the devil. He is destroyed by hot water, but actually thrives in warm water.

You may ask, "How do I get hot and stay hot?" Simply, get any known sin out of your life and turn up the heat of your spiritual passion. There is no devil you cannot conquer. Jesus Christ has given you the power. Christ died to make you an overcomer, and God never sends anyone out to battle without first providing for his or her victory.

And when He had called unto Him His twelve disciples, He gave them power against unclean spirits, to cast them out, and to heal all manner of sickness and all manner of disease (Matthew 10:1).

The gospel that was to be preached to the world was more than just presenting a new philosophy of life. It was to bring the power of God into daily realities. Christ did not send the apostles to merely declare the gospel, but to demonstrate the gospel.

And He said unto them, Go ye into all the world, and preach the gospel to every creature. He that believeth and is baptized shall be saved; but he that believeth not shall be damned. And these signs shall follow them that believe; in my name shall they cast out devils; they shall speak with new tongues; they shall take up serpents; and if they drink any deadly thing, it shall not hurt them; they shall lay hands on the sick, and they shall recover (Mark 16:15-18).

The promise given in the commission to the world for those who would receive Christ was twofold. First, those who believed would be saved. Secondly, those who believed would have power over the enemy. Have you believed on and received the life of Jesus Christ into your life? If so, then you will be saved! That's not all! You have the power to overcome the afflictions and oppositions satan has brought into your life! The latter promise is as real as the former! Those who know that Christ has secured their salvation can be equally assured that He brings them power over all evil spirits and all manner of sickness.

Some in the body of Christ are "sign seekers" looking for a spiritual celebrity. This is not what God intended. For too long people in the pew have looked to the pulpit for the power when, in reality, if the man or woman in the pew truly believes what is being preached, he or she will have the power. Stephen, one of the first deacons, clearly illustrates this truth (see Acts 7). His job was to run a delivery service for the widows, but he had signs and wonders following his bread wagon! You don't have to be a preacher or even have a preacher present to whip the devil in your life. Any true believer, not just a preacher, has the power to overcome! Of course, those preaching are also believers and have signs following their ministries. Just as the glory of the comet is the fiery hot tail that streaks behind it as it races across the heavens, the fire will follow where the gospel is believed! Where the fire of God glows, the devil leaves! He melts in the heat of the good news that Jesus Christ has risen from the dead!

So let's change that "I couldn't care less," lukewarm attitude to an "I couldn't care more" persuasion and whip the devil down to size. Devil shrinking must be done in hot temperatures. Without holy passion that seeks after and surrenders to God, satan will not flee. The manufacturer's label on lucifer says, "Shrinks in hot water." Let's turn up the heat and watch him shrink!

Devil Shrinking 101 is simply this: It can be done! You can do it!

Chapter Two

Who's the Boss?

A Lesson About Fear

I will never forget the day God asked me the question, "Who's in charge?" It happened during a difficult period in my life, when I felt for the first time that I did not want to be a preacher. I thought I wanted out of the ministry and was looking for the nearest exit. I was very tired, depleted, and discouraged. At that time, I had been co-pastoring a church with my husband for more than 20 years. This experience had followed 13 years of traveling across the nation conducting church revivals. Those 33 years, along with motherhood and family responsibilities, had taken a real physical toll on my body. The discouraging experiences and difficult encounters had left a mark on my soul. I found myself asking God if I could just love Him, but not have to put up with His people.

The Lord is wonderful, but he has some difficult children. Like Paul, I felt I bore in my body the marks of the Lord Jesus. This included the wounds and woes of three ministries, which was more than any one heart could handle. I was the daughter of a pastor, I became a preacher and I married a preacher. My whole life had been filled up with ministry. My childhood desire, my teenage endeavor, and my adult vocation had all been one thing and one thing only—ministry. The problem was that I found myself in a weakened condition in which the woes of the ministry were magnified in my mind and the wonders of the gospel were diminished. The agony of the awful had tarnished the awe! My mind was full of misery.

The Crust of Old Wounds

God gives us grace for what we go through. Part of my dilemma was that I was carrying the hurts of three preachers in just one heart. There were old hurts from the years of my father's early pastoring, and then the ministry pains I endured beside my husband. Of course, there were also my own hurts, disappointments and hard times in ministry. Before my marriage, I had traveled with my sister for seven years as a single female preacher. This was not the most accepted role in the Church in those years. As a child, I had literally lived in poverty while my father pioneered several Pentecostal churches. It seemed I studied American history state by state. Even as a child, my perception of people was keen and my heart was pained at attitudes I saw toward the pastor, my father, whom I admired greatly.

Compared to my childhood, the pastoral experience with my husband seemed much more stable. The first few years that we were pastoring, I expected to wake up any day and find that the church had blown up! After five years of peace, though, I settled in and realized a church could go longer than two years without a significant quarrel. In both our pastorates, the Lord placed us in very good churches with many wonderful people. These were sizable churches with fairly substantial realms of impact, especially compared to the congregations of my childhood. We served our first church in northern Ohio for nearly 13 years until we were called to southern Ohio in 1987. Many of our peers looked upon my husband as being a successful pastor and exceptional preacher. Surprisingly, some even expressed their envy at his seeming success and having things "so good." Yet, I had seen him go beyond the call of duty and endure difficult circumstances that no preacher should have to face. My husband, a man with a shepherd's heart, had taken a lot of what I deemed totally unnecessary abuse from "sheep." My sense was that things were out of control and I could not stop the madness. After years of "parsonage training," I chose to internalize all my thoughts and feelings. Years of this piling up had led to implosion. I felt I was at the end of my rope with none left to tie a knot, much less hold on.

Of course, I wasn't factoring in all the physical sickness and surgeries I had gone through, nor was I taking into consideration the stresses of raising a family and normal life changes. I chalked all my woes up to being in the ministry. My thoughts were that if I could just bail out of ministry, all my problems would be over. Was I right? Not really, but the enemy had succeeded at planting this in my mind. After a few months of doing the survival float, I actually thought I was being rescued. I was feeling a bit stronger physically. I had spent much time forgiving and releasing all those I perceived had hurt me in the ministry. God had dealt with my heart and let me know that, I, too, had been an offender. It is much easier to forgive when one realizes her own need for forgiveness. The Lord revealed this to me through the Old Testament passages about setting slaves free. As Israel set slaves free, God told the people to remember that they, too, were once slaves in Egypt.

Shortly after this revelation, I went to the Northeast to preach at a ladies' retreat for a friend of mine. Generally, I would remain after the retreat and preach that weekend at the host church. It was on such a weekend that I was invited to accompany the pastors, a husband and wife team, to an elder's cookout. While others were enjoying fellowship, I was studying people. This was one of my natural skills and it had been honed through much time and experience.

The pastor was a bit nervous and spent a good deal of time making sure our hostess was able to relax. In fact, if the hostess seemed at all distressed, the pastor or his wife would scurry about to fix whatever seemed to be the problem. I sat watching this scenario thinking little of it. After all, this pattern had happened in my home many times before. As they say, "It takes one to know one."

After hamburgers, hot dogs and other common picnic spread, we visited a while and left for the parsonage. It was getting a bit late but I decided to go to the church for a time of prayer and meditation. With any luck, I would come up with something to preach. This had been difficult since my burnout. Passion was obviously at an all-time low, and not too far behind was my physical energy. I entered the door of the little brick church in the woodlands of New England and made my way to the front. The stage was four feet high and steps lined the front forming an altar about the right height for me. I knelt and attempted to talk to God, something I had been reluctant to do for the previous four months. After all, could I really trust God? Hadn't He allowed my total exhaustion and failed to punish my enemies?

It was obvious by now that my desire for doing this job had waned. It took all my remaining courage to just push through the motions. My hope was that somewhere in the process things would change. In fact, I knew they had to change if I were to survive long-term ministry. I had heard of ministry burnout and had friends who had hit bottom and never recovered. I hoped this would not be the case with me. Maybe if I would just "hang in there," God would come through for me. There were moments it seemed I was on an upswing. But just as quickly as those moments came, they vanished and back down the hill I went. It was like a roller coaster except the highs were not *that* high. How could one go so low without the corresponding high peaks? It was a puzzle.

When the Lord spoke to me in this church, it had been another day of going through the motions. I prayed a while and drudged through. I managed to ask God if somehow He could fix my problem. By now I recognized that things would seem to be getting better, but then when the least little problem arose, I wanted to "run away." There were moments that I was not so tuned in to the pain. Yes, I told Him, there were a few sensations of victory, but they were short-lived. As soon as a problem arose again, I wanted back out. Then reality set in. If I didn't conquer this, it was going to bring the worst out in me and the thing I feared the most would happen: I would not last in ministry. Sometimes I wondered if I would last at all. I told God that my heart did not want the world and there wasn't any real temptation to sin, I just wanted to detach from church life.

My time at the altar soon ended and as I started for the door I was stopped by a voice. "Who runs this church?" It was a voice I recognized that asked this unusual question. "Who runs this church?" I was about to answer, "Why the pastor, of course." After all, it seemed he was the person who was most on the ball and this seemed to be the obvious answer. I was just about to leave when I heard more. The voice said, "Not so! Whomever the pastor fears is who is running this place."

Now this was a revelation. I had just watched as the pastors tried so hard to please the elder's wife at the picnic. What a thought! *Whomever one fears is actually in charge.* I whirled around. I hadn't had this kind of revelation in a while and was quite desperate for a Sunday sermon. This was potent. It ought to preach (that's a preacher's term for a good sermon). I proceeded toward the door. *I will let them have it in the morning,* I thought. This was a life-changing revelation for them. Maybe it would be a "better than usual" sermon for me. After all, mine hadn't been too enthusiastic lately. God surely was good to give me insight into their problems!

I was almost out the door when the voice sounded again. This time it was not about them. The Lord asked me, "Who runs you?" *Oh, come on now,* I thought, *surely this was not about to turn personal.* Again, "Who runs you?" Now this was not funny. A truly good sermon was being ruined by a personal question. The question pierced my heart and instantly it melted. I broke and started to cry. Beneath the surface of pain and distress was a heart that really loved the Lord.

For the first time I realized that I had almost let my need for comfort and my dread of confrontation kill the deepest passion of my life and pull me away from the One I loved the most. I had loved God so much that I spent hours with Him as a child. My high school years had been spent in prayer and fasting. My heart was drawn to Him like no other. The passion had been so strong that when other young women were dreaming of careers in business and were preoccupied with charm and guys, my only thoughts were to spend my life totally dedicated to Him. I had wanted no one more than I wanted Him. I had wanted to devote my days to being in His presence. Now, today, I was looking back and drawing back, trying to find a way to distance myself from Him. My fears had taken their toll. They were costing me everything that was once precious to my heart. And they had the potential of costing so much more.

Next I fell on my face and begin to call out, "Oh God, please forgive me and help me understand how to reverse this process. This is not how I want to feel. This is not what I really want.

This is how I have become and how I have responded to pressure. Please help me find my way back to passionate love." The memories flooded my mind. The times I had been in His presence flashed before my eyes. The flame flickered. I hadn't felt a spark in so long. Could I be passionate again? God continued to deal with my broken, cold heart and said, "Dianne, if you will feed your passion and starve your fears you will recover." How I wanted that. "But how, Lord?" I asked.

How to Fan the Flame

God began speaking to me that day and the things I heard would transform my life. He lovingly turned me toward home and it became obvious to me at that moment that I was not alone or forsaken. I just needed answers. How would I recover the passion that had once pulsated inside my heart?

The Lord seemed to be saying to my spirit, "Do the things you did when you were passionate and you will be passionate again. Pray at the altars with people" (something I had begun to leave to other ministers and the congregation). "Go to church more," He continued (I had been finding excuses to leave services and avoid anything I did not have to attend). "Go where you can receive from Me," said the Lord. "If you can't do that at the church you pastor, then find a place where you can receive ministry and go there." I truly responded, "Yes, Lord. I will. I don't know exactly how, but I will do it." The voice continued, "Your spiritual life is your responsibility. You must find a way to be with Me. You must spend time with Me."

During this experience when God asked me, "Who's in charge?" I recalled a sermon I had heard. We had been blessed throughout the years to have had some of the finest preachers in our pulpits. Among these gifted preachers had been Syvelle Phillips, who had preached at several of our missions conferences. One of those "special messages" came back to me. I

19

remembered he had preached about remaining passionate for God. He pointed out that in the Old Testament, the children of Israel were taught to eat a "whole lot of lamb and a little bit of bitter herb." He mentioned the possibility of that balance being lost and people eating too much bitter herb and not enough lamb. His sermon, "Eat the Lamb," was again food for my weary soul because that is exactly what I had done. I had eaten more of the bitter herb than I had of the "Lamb." I had gone through more experiences with people than I had with Jesus. It was all becoming clear. I needed more time with Jesus. The time I gave to people could not be more than I gave to the Lord. I knew if I could get that balance right, I would again feel my lifelong passion for ministry. How I wanted that back again!

The revelation to my spirit continued as the Lord directed me to the Word: "...stir up the gift of God, which is in thee..." (2 Tim. 1:6). I understood this to literally mean to " fan into flame the fire that is in you." This had been the admonition of Paul to Timothy, but it was Rhema to me. I prayed, "Lord, help me fan the flame." God had given me a plan for recovery. In the time of my temptation He had made a way of escape. He had given me a simple, yet powerful, formula for victory. I give to you what He gave to me: "Feed your passion and starve your fears."

When this truth first came to me it was the very revelation I needed. It was the beginning of a full recovery and a new passion for God. It would be a while before I would feel the total impact, but I had begun the road to real recovery. I can say today, "I have never been more passionate about God, His people and His work, in that order." I do remember longing for the "good old days" when I felt closer to the Lord. But that's not the way I feel today! These are the greatest days of my life. I learned how to shrink the devil. I learned to stop feeding him and starve him instead. I learned to feed my spirit man and discovered how to "fan into flame" the spark of life God had put in my heart. I am in awe again with the wonder of the gospel. My burnout devil shrank before my very eyes.

Today, as I travel the world and preach, it is difficult to believe I ever wanted to abandon the gift that God had placed within me. But the powerful reality is that fear has a devastating, paralyzing quality and I was almost its next victim. I am so glad for "the rest of the story," as Paul Harvey would say. Love conquers all and God's love rescued my heart in my deepest hour of need.

My primary advice to anyone struggling with any area of life is to starve your fear. The question, then, is "How does one starve his fear?" First of all, stop spending so much time with people and things that feed your fear. I had spent countless hours with negative people. They would tell me their gloomy prognosis and it would increase anxiety in my heart. They would assassinate the character of others with their words. Listening to these people had me fearing that I would be their next victim. You see, I viewed people as "all-powerful" and felt that my destiny was in their hands. God would later show me that He alone is all-powerful and I that did not need to fear man.

I learned to unplug from people who were driven by fear. It became clear that there had to be a limit on how much time I would devote to these people. Too much of the news media, periodicals, etc., can also feed fear. There must be a limit to the amount of negative material one reads. I unplugged and unhooked from the sources and resources that fed my fear. I cancelled my subscription to "Who's Done What to Whom Lately?" and instead subscribed to The Philippian Way:

And the peace of God, which passeth all understanding, shall keep your hearts and minds through Christ

Jesus. Finally, brethren, whatsoever things are true, whatsoever things are honest, whatsoever things are just, whatsoever things are pure, whatsoever things are lovely, whatsoever things are of good report; if there be any virtue, and if there be any praise, think on these things. Those things, which ye have both learned, and received, and heard, and seen in me, do: and the God of peace shall be with you (Philippians 4:7-9).

The key is to control what dominates your thoughts. Now I realize that neither pastors, nor anyone else for that matter, can totally avoid people and their issues. But they can certainly limit the negative impact. We do have the right and the power to maintain a better balance. I did this by making sure I had positive input during segments of my day. I began to make sure each day ended on a good note by having only positive input before going to sleep. I listened to good music tapes and watched television or videos that fed my spirit. I began attaching myself to the lifeline that God extended in my direction. I got out of the leaky boat and took hold of the lifeline. There is a lifeline being thrown your way too! Grab it and hang on!

Thought control was another key to my victory. One way of controlling our thoughts is to control the input into our minds by the process I mentioned above. Another helpful thing to control thoughts is to renew the mind with the Word of God. I did this by stopping my "stinkin' thinkin'." Faith produces more faith, while fear produces more fear. The time to work on these issues is not during an anxiety attack. One must implement a plan because to fail to plan is to plan to fail. We must plan to have faith and be drawn by love.

So often we think that faith is the opposite of fear. Indeed it is not. The solution for fear is not faith. The solution for fear is love. "There is no fear in love; but perfect love casteth out fear: because fear hath torment. He that feareth is not made perfect in love" (1 Jn. 4:18). "For God hath not given us the spirit of fear; but of power, and of love, and of a sound mind" (2 Tim. 1:7). Both of these references reveal love as the antidote for fear. Love conquers fear because fear cannot exist when it is not fed.

Love Is Stronger

Love is stronger than fear. If that were not so there would be no married people. Every person facing marriage has fears. We are all aware that the person we are marrying is not perfect but something tells us it will work out all right. What is that something? What causes us to rationalize away all the obvious flaws? I suggest it is love.

Likewise, a mother going into the flames of a house to rescue her child is not motivated by faith. She is really afraid. But fear loses its hold at the arousal of love. She does not do what she does in the absence of fear, but rather in spite of it. Love is stronger than fear. Only when your love for God outweighs the thing you fear will you find courage. Courage acts in the face of fear. Courage is fueled by love.

What I fear cannot stand in the face of what I love. My love for God has pulled me through every situation and given me the courage to keep on. His love for me has held me when I could not have held myself. God is love and He is bigger than any problem that you or I will ever have. Our testimony will always be, "Love lifted me!"

Whosoever shall confess that Jesus is the Son of God, God dwelleth in him, and he in God. And we have known and believed the love that God hath to us. God is love; and he that dwelleth in love dwelleth in God, and God in him (I John 4:15-16).

What is God asking you? Who is in charge of your life? What is the ruling force of your private world? May the answer be, "I am at peace, for the One I love is in control!"

Let the peace of God rule in your hearts, to the which also ye are called in one body; and be ye thankful. Let the word of Christ dwell in you richly in all wisdom; teaching and admonishing one another in psalms and hymns and spiritual songs, singing with grace in your hearts to the Lord. And whatsoever ye do in word or deed, do all in the name of the Lord Jesus, giving thanks to God... (Colossians 3:15-17).

When God's love reigns, hearts are at peace!

Chapter Three

The Dirty Dozen

Satan's Evil Tricks

Lucifer's goal is to become like God. Fat chance! About the only way the devil is like God is that he has not changed throughout the years. Satan is no different now than he was when he spoke to Eve in the garden. He has not changed his objectives or his tactics. People are being duped by the same old tricks, so why would he need to change? After all, if you are achieving your goal there is no need for new methods. But what exactly is satan's goal? He has a simple three-fold objective and Christ Jesus exposed this by contrasting the devil to himself.

Then said Jesus unto them again, Verily, verily, I say unto you, I am the door of the sheep. All that ever came before me are thieves and robbers: but the sheep did not hear them. I am the door: by me if any man enter in, he shall be saved, and shall go in and out, and find pasture. The thief cometh not, but for to steal, and to kill, and to destroy: I am come that they might have life, and that they might have it more abundantly (John 10:7-10).

There you have it. The devil is out to steal, kill and destroy. He wants to rob you of life and limb. He has no good intentions for your life. All his plans are evil. In contrast, the plans of the Lord are for good and not for evil, as proclaimed in Jeremiah 29:11. Satan is out to divide and conquer. He is on a search and destroy mission. He has been doing it for centuries and is still doing it today. He is using the same old dirty tricks to steal from people and leave them with damage and decay. What are his common tricks? There are many, but let us consider the "dirty dozen."

1. Accusation

And I heard a loud voice saying in heaven, Now is come salvation, and strength, and the kingdom of our God, and the power of his Christ: for the accuser of our brethren is cast down, which accused them before our God day and night. And they overcame him by the blood of the Lamb, and by the word of their testimony... (Revelation 12:10-11).

Satan is the accuser of the believers. His accusations continue "day and night"—even before the throne of God. Have you ever heard blatant accusations and wondered about their origin? This Scripture should provide insight for you. The enemy of our soul considers accusations an effective tool in defeating his opposition. He accuses us before God both for things we have and have not done.

Vince Wilson, an old mountain preacher and friend of our family, often said, "Satan will tempt you to sin; then when you sin, he will keep it ever before you." This is so true. Satan tries to make our prayers ineffective by reminding us of our past and follows up by declaring that we don't deserve God's provision. He blames us for sins of commission as well as sins of omission. He wants to push us into self-condemnation.

Satan also accuses us before others. If he does it before God in Heaven, we cannot expect less on earth. Often these are false accusations. He brings doubt to the minds of our friends and convincing proof to our enemies. Actually, it may not be proof at all, but those gripped by an accusing spirit will always find the proof they need. Assumptions are often based on weak evidence—but to them, it is proof.

The ninth commandment also gives us insight into the subject of accusation. The actual meaning of this commandment is often interpreted, "Do not lie." But the commandment was "Thou shall not bear false witness..." (see Ex. 20:16). It means do not accuse wrongly or testify falsely against someone. Why this commandment? It was because false charges are of the devil. Job's friends were classic examples of friends who considered circumstantial evidence and drew incriminating conclusions.

Shrink the accuser—ignore him.

2. Anger

Another trap of the enemy is misplaced or mishandled anger. Anger itself is not sin. We all feel angry at times. God is angry at the wicked every day. Anger is not evil, but to misplace it or mismanage it leads to sin. Anger is intended to alert us to a violation. When we feel angry it is our clue that something has happened to us that needs our attention. However, when we do not process it appropriately, it can be harmful.

Anger triggers the flight or fight systems of the body, releasing adrenaline. Anger is a part of the fear cycle. It is composed of fear, frustration, and pain. It gives us energy to fight off an attack or get out of harm's way. It is intended to help us run from or retaliate with our present danger.

But anger can become like a river risen above its banks or a fire out of control. Some people wait until their anger is at unmanageable proportions before they do anything about it. They wait until their anger has turned to rage and then they destroy themselves and others. When that energy is used to attack others, it becomes destructive. Sometimes it is even used to destroy oneself. Suicide is a result of anger turned inward. It is an expression of "others-centered" and "self-centered" contempt.

In controlling our anger, it may help to realize that in this life, there is *stimulus*, then *cognition* and then the *response*. When something happens, that event is the stimulus. We are then to take what happened and filter it through our brain or our cognition. The next step is to initiate our response. The more difficult the situation, the more cognitive thinking we need. Some people do not think long and appear to go straight from the stimulus to the response. This is what we call a short fuse. The key is to spend more time between the two. We need to think and think and think.

We must learn to think before we explode. Then we won't have so much to think about afterward. Anger, like a loaded weapon, must be used with extreme caution. We cannot aim it at others, nor should we put it away loaded. We need skills to unload and separately store the weapon and the ammunition. There is a safe way to handle anger. The Word of God teaches us to "let not the sun go down upon your wrath" (Eph. 4:26). In other words, settle it before sundown. It also teaches that if we have a problem with someone we should go to them and settle it (see Mt. 18:15).

Shrink anger—think control!

3. Bitterness

We are taught to be careful to not let a root of bitterness spring up in us. It will defile us because it is a leftover offense. Some people do not understand how to process offenses. The only real relief to bitterness is forgiveness. Bitterness is like spiritual indigestion—it burns like fire within and leaves a long-lasting bitter taste in our mouths. Just as certain foods can leave a bitter aftertaste, the issues of life can also be bitter. To combat this we must learn the act of forgiveness.

I was always a person to hold grudges, though I was not offended often or easily. Even when there was a deliberate effort on the part of the offender, it was still difficult for me to forgive. Then God revealed to me that unforgiveness was rooted in pride. I had always thought, *Well, I certainly would never commit that sin.* The bottom line was that I would never need forgiveness for that offense, so why should I forgive others? God had to expose my heart and help me realize that I, too, had offended. I needed forgiveness and therefore I must forgive. It was difficult to extend grace to others until I recognized how much grace I needed. An arrogant person holds others in unforgiveness. I know because I, myself, have been arrogant. But I have learned to release others and I do not will to hold them in bondage for the things they do that crush me.

Smith Wigglesworth had an interesting approach to this subject. He took communion every day because he wanted to keep a "short list." That is a great idea. The body and blood of Christ Jesus will help us to keep our list of offenses short and our sins forgiven. It will give us the strength to forgive others and not become bitter at the losses experienced in our life. Bitterness is a faith killer. It condemns our heart and hinders our confidence toward God (see 1 Jn. 3:20-21).

Shrink bitterness—forgive!

4. Conflict

Conflict is inevitable. It is one of satan's greatest schemes. He uses conflict to divide and destroy. Take note that all of the dirty tricks satan plays are destructive. He does nothing to build up or exhort. Conflict can also include traces of anger, bitterness and much of the other rubbish he manufactures. Conflict is also caused by pride. With pride comes contention and every evil work. Conflict, like other things, is not in itself sin nor does it have to be destructive. It is when it is not appropriately handled that it brings devastation. James chapter 4 gives the origins of these things. He further tells us that they come from unsatisfied lust, something we will look at later.

But what a concept! Conflict is a result of "blocked goals." When someone gets in the way of something we want, there is conflict. We use the term "conflict of interest." Actually, all conflict is a conflict of interest—your interest vs. someone else's interest. Conflict is often driven by misunderstanding. Paul says in 1 Corinthians chapter 3 that these conflicts originate from being carnal. Carnality and lust do go hand in hand. Fussing, fighting, dividing, and mud-throwing all are temper fits in which adults indulge. We would discipline our children for such behavior, but we allow these things to exist in our own lives. God wants us to grow up and to be one, even as He and the Father are One (see Jn. 17:22).

Shrink conflict—promote understanding!

5. Deception

Let's look at the fifth dirty trick the devil uses, deception. Deception is a slippery slope. It looks inviting but is not as it seems. Satan will appear as an angel of light. He will look like a sheep, but in reality he is a wolf. He goes to great lengths to deceive. The Scriptures tell us that Eve was deceived (see

Gen. 3). So we see that even in the beginning, deception was used to bring destruction to the human race.

Deception is generally built on half-truths. It would be very difficult to deceive without some truth being presented. The problem is that a half-truth is actually a lie. Deception is developed in distortion. It is just slightly out of shape. You can almost see clearly, but not quite. As a child I remember being fascinated by the distorted mirrors in amusement parks. Some mirrors made you look short and fat while others made you look tall and thin. I spent a considerable amount of time there trying to get the exact shape I wanted, but it didn't help. I will never be tall and thin. Nevertheless, it was a distortion.

Likewise, satan doesn't peddle his goods with facts. His selling points are twisted figures and distorted concepts. Our pursuit for truth must be unending. We need to buy the truth and sell it not, just as we are admonished to do in Scripture (see Prov. 23:23). The truth brings freedom—but deception leads to destruction and bondage. For example, no one in her right mind would become an alcoholic or a drug addict if the whole truth were understood beforehand. People are lulled in by deception, by hearing things such as, "This chemical will solve your problem." Or, "You will feel better if you try a little of this." And let's not forget, "All your friends do it, you will be left out of the group if you don't do what we do." These are the devil's prime selling points.

Shrink deception—love truth!

6. Discouragement

If satan cannot stop you from trying, he will try to stop you from succeeding. He'll just move to the sidelines and try to discourage you. Discouragement is the act of disheartening a person. Nehemiah faced this sort of hassle. The enemies of God stood on the ground and tried to discourage him by shouting demeaning remarks. They said a fox would cause the wall to fall (see Neh. 4:3). Belittling and berating remarks come from the devil. He is the master of discouragement.

Satan works to undermine your faith and weaken your determination. He gloats when you allow him to sap your victory. He will do anything to slow you down or knock you out. Paul said it best when satan attacked him with discouragement, "I am knocked down, but not knocked out" (see 2 Cor. 4:9). He further confirmed that the things coming against us cannot stop us but will only work for our benefit and the end result will be a "...far more exceeding and eternal weight of glory" (2 Cor. 4:17).

I try to keep the perspective Paul had and when the enemy attacks me I exercise the "Billy Goat Gruff" defense. Here's how it works: Say, "Oh, you don't really want to whip me. There is a great big guy coming along after a while." Then sit back and watch as "Big Brother" Jesus takes on the already defeated devil!

God gives courage to the faint. He gives strength when we need it. Shrink discouragement by applying a generous amount of "bootstrap" therapy. I know you are asking, "What is 'bootstrap therapy'?" It is when you take hold of the tabs on both sides of your own boots and give a big tug! David encouraged himself in the Lord and we must do the same (see 1 Sam. 30:6). Don't wait for someone to come by to help. Just think of the Scriptures, songs and other encouraging things you know and get out of that rut. I have what I call a "spiritual I.V. (intravenous) pack." It's a library of books, tapes, CD's, videos, letters of encouragement, poetry, etc., that I use to give myself a boost when I feel discouragement settling in. Remember, it is easier to get out of the hole when you first fall in than to wait until you are in too deep. Some people dig instead of climb. Do not lie down in discouragement. Get up! Get out! Get going!

Shrink discouragement—
encourage yourself

7. Distraction

If you want to know exactly what distraction is, just think of all the things that have happened while you were trying to read this book. You may not have known you had a telephone until you began reading. Distraction is a bit like dis...track... ion. Getting you off track is satan's goal.

Prayer time is a big target of the enemy's. Just begin praying and he will remind you of all the things you could never remember to do. You may have thought you had "old-timer's disease," but when you start praying, your memory will suddenly perk up. Try studying the Word of God and distraction will come again. I have also found that one of the battles with distraction is that it tempts you to expend your energies on things that are unproductive.

Shrink distraction—focus!

8. Intimidation

In the story of David and Goliath (see 1 Sam. 17), Goliath was intimidating the people of God. He was using his size as well as his voice to taunt them. I love the contrast God makes here. He sent a small man to defeat Goliath and used a small weapon for the devastating blow! A young man who knew how to use a slingshot and whose heart had been worshiping God, delivered the fatal blow. God answered this giant with accuracy and courage.

The enemy wants you to shake in your boots and run and hide behind the hills, but God will give you courage to *run to your victory*. The purpose of intimidation is to scare you. No wonder God said to Jeremiah, "Be not afraid of their faces..." (Jer. 1:8). God also said, "I have put my words in thy mouth..." (Is. 51:16a). When God's words are in your mouth you need not be intimidated!

Shrink intimidation—know your God!

9. Isolation

Isolation is another scheme of satan. He generally does not single out groups of people; he likes to isolate you and then attack. This is the old trick of catching the sick and weak and pouncing on them. The Scripture in Ecclesiastes 4:10 warns, "...woe to him that is alone when he falleth...." We may feel alone, but we are never truly alone. God is always with us.

We are to be insulated but not isolated. Jesus said we are "in the world" although we are not "of the world" (see Jn. 17). We must stay connected to the Body of Christ so we don't become a target, get singled out and attacked. If we do we'll be like a chunk of coal when taken from the company of others—we will burn out.

We are admonished to come together as believers. We need each other. It is easy to be discouraged and want to pull away into our shell, but this will result in our destruction. We must stay visibly attached to believers. John was on an island but God did not leave him alone. He had plenty of company. An orchestra, angels, animals and all came to his rescue. And then there was the man among the candlesticks (see Rev. 1:13). That's what happens when one tries to banish a child of God. Even Jesus is the "Lord of hosts." He does not travel alone but stays surrounded with angels. The Word tells us that we, too, are surrounded by angels. It takes more than one angel to "encamp about" me. It takes three people to gather "around."

Stephen was not alone during the stoning. Daniel was not alone in the den of lions. God will never leave us or forsake us (see Heb. 13:5).

We must work to stay connected to other believers. We cannot afford to let petty opinions and divisive things separate us from each other.

Shrink isolation—fellowship!

10. Lust

Another tool of the enemy is lust. Lust is a natural desire that is wrongly focused. God placed the desire for food in Adam and Eve. He created food for them to eat. The problem arose when they turned their desire to the forbidden fruit. Lust wants the wrong things while pure desire wants the right things. Lust also comes into play when we crave more than our share or more than what is good for us. Gluttony and greedy eyes are never satisfied. The lust for "things, things, and more things" becomes a trap into which far too many people fall. Lust can further be defined as a desire that is out of bounds or a need that is out of control.

We often use the word *lust* in referring to sexual sin. Sex was God's idea; it is natural and can be a good thing in our lives. Lust, on the other hand, is destructive. The world uses sex appeal to market just about anything these days. Yet, the craving will never be satisfied by what it is selling. A beer advertisement is a perfect example. Often it is presented to tap into sexual desire, but the drunkard does not wind up with a pretty girl. Instead, he may lose his wife, destroy his kids, or even take innocent lives in an accident. He loses and destroys the very things he wanted to get in the first place. The problem with lust is that it shows us one thing, but always delivers another.

Shrink lust—be content!

11. Shame

The enemy uses shame or disgust to negate our spiritual life. Shame-based Christians are hindered in their effectiveness. Many people within the Church today, like those around them in the world, are filled with toxic shame. They are poisoned with feelings of being unworthy of any good thing. These feelings of being worthless or not as good as others are at the foundation of their belief system. These wrong feelings affect every aspect of their lives as well as their relationships with others. There is a reason Christ taught us to love others as we love ourselves. It is simply because we cannot love others unless we love ourselves. We cannot accept others unless we accept ourselves.

Christ came to set us free from shame. We don't have to be ashamed because Jesus bore our shame. Christ is the lifter of our head (see Ps. 3:3). He will give us courage to face the world. Yes, all have sinned, but in Christ we are justified by our faith in His life, death, and resurrection.

Looking unto Jesus the author and finisher of our faith; who for the joy that was set before Him endured the cross, despising the shame, and is set down at the right hand of the throne of God (Hebrews 12:2).

Shrink shame—receive forgiveness!

12. Unbelief

Finally, the devil uses unbelief to trick us. It does not take a Hebrew or Greek scholar to understand this word. Either we believe or we do not believe. Unbelief will always limit and often eliminate our faith in God. Unbelief begins with doubt. The first thing satan did when tempting Eve was to cast doubt on what God had said. Doubting the word of God leads to unbelief and unbelief is sin. It leaves people in a spiritual wilderness, unable to come into their promised land.

> *For some, when they had heard, did provoke: howbeit not all that came out of Egypt by Moses. But with whom was He grieved forty years? Was it not with them that had sinned, whose carcases fell in the wilderness? And to whom sware He that they should not enter into His rest, but to them that believed not? So we see that they could not enter in because of unbelief* (Hebrews 3:16-19).

Unbelief is the opposite of faith. The Book of Hebrews teaches us about faith. It tells us faith is essential to pleasing God. "Without faith it is impossible to please Him: for he that cometh to God must believe that He is, and that He is a rewarder of them that diligently seek Him" (Heb. 11:6). The devil knows that unbelief will cause us to doubt the existence of God. Unbelief will cause us to believe God isn't benevolent. Satan leaves us thinking God won't reward our seeking after Him. Unbelief then robs us of the blessings that were reserved for us. Satan tricks us into not believing the truth. He knows that in order for us to believe the lie, we have to first doubt the truth. Eve doubted the truth of what God had said, which set her up to believe the lie of the devil, "ye shall not surely die" (Gen. 3:4).

Shrink unbelief—believe God!

I trust that after these first three chapters, the devil is needing to order a new suit. If perhaps the clothes he wore when you began to read this book are a few sizes too large, keep reading, it's working!

Chapter Four

MOUSE HUNT

A Story of Determination

We live in the country on a few acres of land. The sunset paints the sky to tuck us in at night and its hot glaring beams awaken us in the mornings. There are many blessings to living in the country. I love the rolling hills of Ohio. I relax while watching for deer on the seven-mile country drive home from our church. I love the freedom to sing (my neighbors appreciate the acreage) and I prefer to pray aloud to God. God seems so close out in the country. I enjoy riding a four-wheeler, walking country lanes and even mowing grass. These all are blessings of rural living.

As one might suspect, though, there is another side to living in the country. Yes, there is beauty and blessing, but there are also beasts and pests. And try as you might, it is impossible to insulate yourself from these critters since any quarter-inch opening is like a garage door to them. There is a Scripture that says spiders invade kings' palaces; mice have been found living in mine.

HONEY, I SHRUNK THE DEVIL!

This story begins when I was sitting in the lower level of my home trying to relax by watching something really boring on television. I decided that to watch *CNN Headline News* for the second time around qualified as boring.

As I sat there glued to the screen, out of the corner of my eye I saw a flash of something dark scooting along the floor. Denial was immediate: *Oh, that can't be. Surely, I have an eye problem and am seeing things.* A few moments later the same thing occurred, but the flash was going the opposite direction. *This can't just be an eye problem,* my brain now made the intelligent assumption. *That could be a mouse I am seeing.* Now this didn't come as a total shock. After all, I do live in the country. It was fall and field mice are known to seek inside shelter at this time of year. However, even with that bit of information, I was still rationalizing to myself that "this is a new home" and it "must be a freak discrepancy in my vision." No one wants to believe critters are invading her world. With that sense of false security, I drifted off for a brief nap in the middle of the afternoon.

A few days later, I retreated to the family room again in the lower level of my home. I sat on the couch and put my feet up on the glass coffee table. I was a bit more relaxed than usual as I flipped through the channels and came upon something interesting enough to hold my attention. But it wasn't stimulating enough to get my adrenaline going and keep me awake. After all, I came down here to relax and rest. While sitting there, I was suddenly distracted by something gray and furry running right under my feet between the sofa and the coffee table. Now denial was cracking and reality was knocking. *Dianne, you've got a mouse in this basement,* my brain informed me. *There is NO doubt, that is a mouse!*

Now, I am one who becomes the calm kind of excited. I felt a bit unnerved at the idea of having a mouse cohabiting with me, but I didn't jump onto the table and scream as I know some of my contemporaries would have done. However, my comfort had been disturbed. I really don't like mice. After all, mice in the house are an "abomination." They are filthy and should never be tolerated. I decided to use "pest control" and get rid of them. Of course, my brand of "pest control" does not include calling a professional exterminator. I felt quite adequate in this area as I was raised in the country and have had a lot of experience with these critters.

In the days that ensued, I purchased all the necessary paraphernalia and went about the job of ridding my house of its latest intruders. I thought the old cheese recipe and a few traps should do, so I baited a few and set them around the walls of my normally relaxing room. It was somewhat disconcerting to come into a room to rest and have to see all those open traps about the walls, but this was how it had to be because catching this mouse was imperative. A few days passed and nothing happened. Nothing, that is, except that the little critter got up the nerve to run under my legs again. So much for my peaceful resting place. It had now become a war zone and I was determined to win!

Contemplating what could be delaying my effectiveness, I began to rationalize. Perhaps this was not a cheese-loving mouse in my house. Perhaps this little fellow would prefer peanut butter. I had heard peanut butter is a delicacy in the mouse kingdom, so with that in mind, I carefully collected and triggered each trap. The cheese menu was now gone and peanut butter skillfully applied. *There, that should do it*, I thought. *They will surely love Jiffy Smooth.* I listened that evening hoping to hear the loud click of victory as my furry friend ventured to fill his hunger. But no click came. Once again, I was outwitted. I was gradually becoming discouraged with the process. I hadn't actually seen the fellow in the last several days. So I told myself I didn't have to be in a hurry and I became a bit complacent. Still, my intentions were to get that mouse, but I reasoned, *He is in the basement, not on the main floor or in the kitchen or upstairs bedrooms. And after all, he hasn't hurt anything; he is just a pest.*

Well, time passed and spring was fast approaching. Each year in March, I host a women's conference and this year I had friends coming to stay with me. I had plenty of room: a full basement with its own apartment-size kitchen, bath and a big bedroom with two queen-size beds. I did have one slight problem: My guests were women, and the screaming kind at that. Realizing this, I knew I must get rid of the mouse on that floor, if for no other reason than as a courtesy to my friends. This situation provided the needed impetus for me to again institute my project and plan the "de mice" of my furry intruder.

It was much more urgent now. I really had a deadline for getting rid of this creature. I owed it to my friends to get rid of the mouse before they came. Furthermore, I did not intend to inform them that there had been one. I wanted them to be able to rest in my basement and doubted they could if they knew there had ever been a mouse there.

Rethinking my strategy, I decided that if cold cuts and peanut butter were not the winning meal, then perhaps I should cook. My husband remarked that I did not even cook for him. Nonetheless, I fried bacon and again went through the trap-setting process. I wiped off the peanut butter, inserted the bacon and reset the spring. The smell of freshly fried bacon made even *my* mouth water. I was sure to catch that mouse. May I say in hindsight, though, I don't think the menu counts in mouse catching. I suspect it is more a matter of determination to get rid of the pest.

Shortly after that, I was sitting comfortably on my sofa enjoying being bored by the third trip around the world with CNN. Then something caught my eye. Beside me on the sofa was an afghan someone had given me. And to my utter shock and amazement, perched on top of the afghan, was that mouse. "That's it! That's it! I have had it! You have gone too far! Today is the day you will die!" I said.

Up I came off that couch. Adrenaline rushed through every vein of my body. I quickly went into my "emergency mouse killing mode." Up the stairs I flew, and into the pantry where I keep my cleaning supplies. I grabbed my broom and descended the stairs. Every cell in my body was on alert and my Essary (maiden name) blood was now pumping, preparing me for one of the greatest confrontations I had ever faced. I was a woman with a mission. I was determined and I would not be denied. "Today is the day! Mr. Mouse, you have been here too long. You have botched up my rest time and run freely in my house. You have become bolder and more aggressive as time has passed and now you are beside me on the couch! You have pressed your luck too far!" I yelled.

I tried to imagine where I would go if I were a mouse, and pictured where I could corner him so he couldn't escape. I closed every door and began a systematic cleansing of the basement— starting first with the afghan. I pulled it up, shook it out, and threw it back on the sofa. Next, I picked up each cushion and shook it. I looked into the corners and then moved the coffee table, reaching for the handle to unfold the sofa bed. I gave a powerful yank and unfolded the bed while emptying the furry little pest onto the floor! It jumped up and began scurrying about the room. Behind him I bolted in hot pursuit. Broom in hand, raised into the air and ready to strike, I ran wildly around the basement. But I lost sight of him. I checked under the recliner and on the bookshelves. I finally concluded that he had left that room for the recreation room directly adjacent it.

After checking every possible spot, I narrowed it to one place where he had to be. We had a drum set that my son, Sean, had set up in the room. To muffle the sound, he had placed an old orange quilt inside the bass drum. That was where Mr. Mouse had to be. I reached inside the drum and pulled out the quilt. I shook it, and sure enough, the mouse hit the floor with a thud and then scurried away. Behind him I ran, broom ready to strike. I came within striking distance, lowered the broom, and dazed my target. He wobbled to his feet and started up the brick fireplace wall in the family room. I reached up with my broom and gave him a whomp. He staggered, but kept running. So I ran after him. Whomp, whomp! Whomp! I was now hitting my target with great fervor. You would have thought I was attacking an African bull elephant. My muscles were over-working and my anxiety level had peaked. One more whomp and I was done! Then the Lord called the poor thing home!

Panting and exhausted, I reached over and grabbed the tail of my defeated foe. Lifting him to eye level, I felt a sense of satisfaction and then disgust as I looked at the nasty, furry creature I had let stay too long. Yes, that day I was the victor. I opened the door onto the lower patio and went outside. I gave him a toss back into the ecology system from whence he came. Without even a formal burial, he was gone.

This long, detailed story may appear to have little relevance to devil shrinking. But in reality, it has all the relevance in the world. It is a classic demonstration of "why we do" and "why we don't" get rid of the pest that invades our soul. We will never get rid of the devil until we are *determined* to do so.

You may be thinking, as I was in the beginning, *Oh well, I know how to get rid of that. I can stop smoking pot, running around with the wrong crowd, viewing filthy magazines, spreading gossip or destructive thinking. But it is no big deal for now. I will do it when I need to.* Let me tell you, you are playing with an aggressive foe and he will gain momentum unless you determine to take action! You must get fed up with the enemy of your soul. Injuring him is not sufficient. He must be mortally wounded. Stop the denial and face the facts. The devil has run loose in your life for too long. Perhaps all he is doing is disturbing your rest, but you will never get rid of him without a lot of determination.

The children of Israel were instructed to utterly destroy their enemies (see Deut. 7:2). And if they didn't destroy them, the enemies would become pricks in their eyes and thorns in their sides (see Num. 33:55). These Scriptures give us the basis for destroying the work of the enemy in our life. We must make a "clean sweep" or we will be left with frustration and trouble. It takes a lot of will power to utterly destroy the enemy. But strongholds will be broken when we make up our mind to complete the task. We may set a trap or two, or even intend to rid ourselves of the pest, but the job will be accomplished only when we add determination.

Sometimes there are delays in ridding ourselves of "the pest." This happens when we have a double mind. We sort of want deliverance, and we fool ourselves into thinking we are doing our best. But we are still providing for the flesh. We can't leave holes in the walls and drop food onto the floor and expect to get rid of mice. Likewise, we can't leave holes in our souls and feed our flesh and expect the devil to leave us alone. If we make provision for the flesh, the flesh will thrive and the spirit will die. "A double minded man is unstable in all his ways"

45

(Jas. 1:8). Wishy washy Christianity won't get the job done. We must determine in our minds and our hearts to be victorious.

Too often we placate the devil. We tolerate petty sins and excuse ourselves in our failures. We look for ways not to be discovered instead of ways to be free. We hide our sins in hopes we will not be found out. We aren't alarmed until we realize company is coming and there is potential for embarrassment. When we come to our senses, we know we must exterminate the enemy. Sometimes the damage is already done. We may kill the mouse but if the nest is already full of babies, we will reap the fruit of our delay.

Mice tracks should be enough to alarm us. I don't know why I didn't pick up on the early warnings. Like so many, I was not observant until the obvious happened. My prayer is that God will increase our sensitivity to intruders of our hearts. May we be disturbed and spring into action long before the enemy takes over.

Getting rid of the devil and his impact in our lives will require tenacity. We can't pet him for a while and then decide we want him to leave. The first signs of transgression should be all we need. We must understand that the end of lust is death, and therefore we cannot give in and we cannot give up. We must complete the task of totally destroying the works of the devil in our lives!

Chapter Five

Hit the Road, Jack

Total Eviction

As we mentioned briefly in the previous chapter, the Book of Numbers instructs the children of Israel to drive their enemy out of the land God has given them (see Num. 33:55). God further states that those inhabitants not driven out will become pricks in their eyes, thorns in their sides and shall vex them in the land wherein they dwell. God gave His people the concept of totally evicting the enemy. In the Bible narrative, God used the terms "dispossess" and "possess." We must understand the process of dispossessing the enemy, because often we must dispossess before we can possess. We must evict or drive out evil before we can possess the good. We must tell satan, "Hit the road, Jack, and don't come back no more, no more, no more!"

How does the concept of total eviction work in the life of the believer? What is the importance of not allowing the devil a foothold? How does he plot his way into the believer's life in the first place? It is my hope you will find practical answers to these questions in this chapter and that the insights shared will enable you to serve an eviction notice to satan.

When coming to Christ we must be serious about destroying the works of satan in our lives. Don't tolerate a half-hearted conversion or accommodate small grievances satan attempts to develop. I have seen people come to the Lord appearing to give Him their whole heart. But, in reality, they were not making a total surrender. These people would pray at the altar but still maintain old, destructive habits. They did not totally drive out the enemy. They refused to address issues that the Holy Spirit exposed to them in their hearts. Ultimately, this resulted in a return to the old lifestyle. This tolerating of "little foxes" or small sins is a familiar scheme satan uses to keep us trapped.

I once watched a young man with a serious drug addiction give his heart to God in a moment of desperation. But he failed in his new walk because he would not sever relationships tied to his addiction. He seemed sincere and attended church for a while. He came to the altar and continued to pray for a time. But little by little he slipped back into old patterns. He thought he was strong enough to maintain friendships with the buddies he had before he became a Christian. But this man did not fill his heart with God's Word or reinforce his life with wholesome relationships. Sure, he did all right for a while, but in a moment of frustration he returned to his old habit. The hole he left in his life was the hole he fell into during his moment of weakness. The ties he failed to sever drew him back to his old master and to sin.

As illustrated above, we absolutely cannot leave any room for the devil in our lives. We must evict him! I'm sure by now it is obvious that I do not see satan as the landlord of our lives, nor do I see him able to invade whomever or wherever he desires. I see him as a bum. But there are those who continually allow themselves to be victimized by satan. They do not seem to even recognize that devil evicting is possible. Well, I am here to enlighten you with the truth—you can evict the devil!

You may ask, "How does satan gain entrance into my life in the first place?" Often, he gains access and settles into our hearts without our recognizing it. Let me explain it like this: You hear a knock on the door and discover that someone has come to visit. You answer the door, have a brief conversation and then become distracted for a time. The next thing you know this visitor is bringing in a suitcase. You are shocked by his assertiveness but don't want to cause a scene or make him feel bad, so you just let him come on in. You think, *I guess he is staying overnight.* But the next day, without permission, he goes out to the vehicle and brings in another suitcase. You still don't find the courage to ask what is going on, so the third day he returns with yet another suitcase. By now you recognize you are being invaded, but you still won't approach the subject of why this person is here. Finding little or no resistance, your uninvited guest perceives kindness as weakness and moves in.

Your guest begins by staying in one room overnight, but the next thing you know he has put his things in your bathroom. Then he leaves a few things in the living room, and finally you look around one day only to realize he is living with you. It is not a visit as you first thought; it is a takeover. He has come to stay. You did not realize what was happening until he was already in the house and settled. Gradually he took over—one corner at a time, one room at a time, one moment at a time...and then a lifetime! He is controlling your life.

Similarly, a young couple told me about a relative that was coming to stay with them for six months. They had agreed to let the relative stay while she looked for a place of her own. "After all, it was just for six months," they said. That six months has now turned into years. The ironic thing is these people don't know how to tell her she must move out. Once she was in the door and her belongings were in place, they did not have the nerve to ask her to leave. How often is this scenario repeated by well-meaning people? While I admit this relative is not the devil, she is using the same tactic. Give him a little encouragement and he will move in; show him kindness and you will find him claiming the family name.

Few of us recognize what is happening when satan moves in. We think having one adverse thought is harmless. We believe we can keep a little bitterness "as an overnight guest." Little do we know we are about to operate a boarding house where we will be keeping, feeding and sleeping with the devil.

In one of my speaking conferences, a lady testified she had been having thoughts about what it would be like to get rid of her husband. She would fantasize about being with other men, movie stars, etc., and would wish she were not married to "her man." Little by little her affections were being stolen by satan and her home was being destroyed. As I preached this truth, she was set free and testified about how God had restored her love for her husband. Thank God she was touched by the Holy Spirit and restored before it was too late.

How does the devil get in? We allow access to the devil when we allow "little sins" to visit our hearts. We give legal access by harboring grievances. It may be just a bit of unforgiveness, but it is enough space for the devil to put his foot in the door. Our heart becomes his home. We can't get rid of him because we have accepted his suitcases that are filled with bitterness, envy, strife, jealousy, hatred, emulation, and other junk. But you say, "He only brought in an overnight case with a little jealousy." Yes, but there was much more in the car. When you treated him nice the first hour, that was his cue that you would tolerate him. What a mistake! When he comes knocking on your door, be aware of his bold, aggressive plan and declare, "Hit the road, Jack, and don't you come back! " Any sign of welcome, any pity, any sense of agreement, gives him permission to stay. We must let him know in no uncertain terms that he is not welcome in our heart.

I once heard of a man who cut off his dog's tail. A friend asked him why he cut the dog's tail. He replied, "I have kin folks coming and I don't want any sign of welcome." Well, that's the type of "de-tailed" attention you must show the devil. Cut him off. Show him that he is not welcome—not even for a moment.

When you tell satan you don't want him, you must make him understand that goes for all the evil he carries as well. All his baggage must go with him or he will be back. You cannot hold on to a bag of bitterness and expect satan to stay away. Any evil thing harbored will be an open invitation for his return. You have heard the old adage, "I left my bag at your house." Satan has too, so in the door he returns! You think he is just there to retrieve his goods, but no! He has all his suitcases in the car. You see, he is a vagabond and just needs a room "for the night." But one night becomes a week, which becomes one year, and then a lifetime. See the progression? He isn't good-mannered nor does he get his feelings hurt and leave. If you want to evict the devil, you must know your rights. You need to get fed up with his aggression into your life, stand in the authority of Christ, and completely evict him!

Scripture mentions a man who was delivered of the devil. His house was swept and garnished but he failed to fill it with a new guest. So when the devil returned, he found "his room" empty and clean. He rounded up some of his buddies and then came back to stay. (See Matthew 12:43-45.) That is exactly how satan still works today. He doesn't come by himself but he takes the liberty to invite friends over for pizza and drinks. The only real way to get rid of the devil is to invite someone else to occupy the room. Jesus is a wonderful house guest! If you give Jesus the room, the devil will leave. Satan will not share a room with Christ. Satan cannot stay. So just force him out with Jesus' occupation and you can be sure of his immediate departure (see Jas. 4:7). A life dedicated to God reveals a "no vacancy" sign to satan. What a revelation!

While this all seems so simple, many of us still are not aware of the extensive damage satan does while he visits. If we only realized we were being intruded upon, I believe we would not tolerate him. Think about this: Would you let an intruder just hang around? Would you feed him and sit around and laugh with him? Would you let him have control of your day? Would you let him choose which channels to watch on television? Would you let him control your thought life? Well, if you have given the devil a room that is exactly what is happening. That is how satan works. His tactics are so contrary to those of the Lord Jesus Christ.

You see, Christ stands at the door, knocks and waits to be invited into the house (see Rev. 3:20). He seeks a welcome and says "up front" that He wants to abide with you. He will not stay where He is not welcome. God will not live where evil crowds Him. If He gets the feeling He is not wanted, He will gently bow out. He will grieve and mourn over the loss of your companionship, but He will not force Himself upon you. This is how Jesus lives while He's in your house. But satan is quite different. He is aggressive, pushy and does not care about you or your property. He never considers what is best for you. He is angry and his goal is to rule and ruin your life. But don't fear, for he can't do that without your permission and cooperation.

But if you do permit and cooperate, not only will the devil move in and stay without a real welcome, he will rip you off. He steals. He will take things without your realization. Before you know it your joy and peace will be gone. You will wonder, "Where is my joy? Where is my peace?" And soon you will realize that satan caught you unaware and ripped you off. You see, satan is sneaky. He will steal from you while you are not spiritually alert. He will wait until you are too busy fussing with a spouse or complaining about your neighbor. Or he'll wait until you are involved gratifying the lusts of the flesh and then carry your virtue out the door. Satan will steal the things most precious to life and dearest to your heart if you give him any place at all. You have heard the expression, "If you give him an inch, he will take a mile." That's the devil's mode of operation.

Satan is a destroyer and don't forget it! He will cover the walls with graffiti and destroy the house. He is not an owner so he will not occupy with an owner's mentality. He will just use the place and destroy it, leaving you with a heap of ashes. Then he will move on to his next victim. How many young minds has he destroyed with LSD or other drugs of lasting impact? How many homes have been broken because of him? Oh, the destruction and devastation that follow the tornado of satan! He leaves behind him a wide, barren path of ruin.

If you really want your heart to have joy, your mind to have peace and your life to have meaning, you must evict the devil! You ask, "How do I evict him?" Well, you start by recognizing that he lives with you. If you are still confused and denying his residency at your place, you won't be able to kick him out. If you continue to make excuses for why he is there, you will not get rid of him. If you become angry when your friends tell you they think he has taken over your life, you won't move him out.

Recognize what has happened and resolve to do something about it.

To obtain a legal eviction notice you must know the rights of the landlord and those of the occupant. You must always follow due process. It is an absolute necessity to know who owns the property. Decide now if you belong to God or to the devil. Once you know you belong to God, you can legally serve the devil an eviction notice. You will have the right to say, "Hit the road, Jack!"

Isn't it time you served the devil an "eviction notice"?

Chapter Six

The Boys Are Back in Town

Creating the Point of No Return

Once you evict the devil, don't relax too much because your work is not over. It is not enough to just get him out. You must keep him out! And in fact, sometimes when you have finally gotten rid of him, it seems like before you know it he has returned with a vengeance. It may appear as though your devil shrinking tactics aren't working at all. Before we go any farther, let's look at several eye-opening verses from the Bible that pertain to gaining and maintaining power over the devil.

And when He was come out of the ship, immediately there met Him out of the tombs a man with an unclean spirit, who had his dwelling among the tombs; and no man could bind him, no, not with chains: because that he had been often bound with fetters and chains, and the chains had been plucked asunder by him, and the fetters broken in pieces: neither could any man tame

*him. And always, night and day, he was in the moun-
tains, and in the tombs, crying, and cutting himself
with stones. But when he saw Jesus afar off, he ran
and worshipped him, and cried with a loud voice, and
said, What have I to do with thee, Jesus, Thou Son of
the most high God? I adjure thee by God, that Thou torment me not. For He said unto him, Come out of the
man, thou unclean spirit. And He asked him, What is
thy name? And he answered, saying, My name is
Legion: for we are many. And he besought him much
that He would not send them away out of the country.
Now there was there nigh unto the mountains a great
herd of swine feeding. And all the devils besought Him,
saying, Send us into the swine, that we may enter into
them. And forthwith Jesus gave them leave. And the
unclean spirits went out, and entered into the swine:
and the herd ran violently down a steep place into the
sea, (they were about two thousand;) and were choked
in the sea. And they that fed the swine fled, and told it
in the city, and in the country. And they went out to see
what it was that was done. And they come to Jesus,
and see him that was possessed with the devil, and had
the legion, sitting, and clothed, and in his right mind:
and they were afraid. And they that saw it told them
how it befell to him that was possessed with the devil,
and also concerning the swine* (Mark 5:2-16).

This story is quite dramatic and there are many insights
that can be gained from the details. For example, the man
had a legion of demons, more than enough to fill 2,000 pigs.
(Perhaps the first-ever deviled ham?) In comparing the man
to one of the pigs, we see that the pig was not willing to live
with fewer devils than the man let live in him for many years.
We also see that, per head, it took fewer demons to destroy an

animal than it did to destroy a human. Is this due to our higher nature and power of will? Perhaps, but the main message to receive from this story is that demons will go somewhere when they are cast out. Their desire to go into something living is obvious from this Bible passage. Devils do not just disappear. The demons in the earth today are the same demons who have been loose on earth since the time of Adam and Eve. Remember, demons are former angels who rebelled and they have all existed longer than the human race. When a person who has demons within him dies, the devils move out looking for a new home. Evil spirits may find a new heart to occupy, but they are the same devils that controlled another being in generations past.

When demons depart from a person, they look for a new body to occupy. They gain their entry through any area of weakness their prey has. In their search for a place to dwell, they will always check out an "old address" to see if they are again welcome. The teaching of Jesus Christ makes this very clear:

When the unclean spirit is gone out of a man, he walketh through dry places, seeking rest, and findeth none. Then he saith, I will return into my house from whence I came out; and when he is come, he findeth it empty, swept, and garnished. Then goeth he, and taketh with himself seven other spirits more wicked than himself, and they enter in and dwell there: and the last state of that man is worse than the first..." (Matthew 12:43-45).

It is common for vagabonds and social outcasts to live in empty buildings. This is true spiritually and socially. Animal predators of the earth are eventually pushed into the wilderness where people do not dwell. So, the demon world has learned to seek out an empty heart or soul in the wilderness of life. This is why it is so important that those who are delivered replace their former occupant, the one they evicted, with a new occupant—the Lord Jesus Christ. The house of the heart cannot be left vacant. It will be filled with something or someone. This principle is not only true for the demon possessed, it is true for people demonized in any way. It also plays an important part in the lives of Christians desiring to move from carnality into spirituality. This principle is also known as the spiritual *law of substitution* and it must be understood and applied. Whenever something is removed, it must be replaced. All vacuums will be filled, but people can determine what and who will fill them.

I want to explain this principle a bit further. Let's say someone was watching pornographic movies ten hours per week and suddenly decides he wants to improve his quality of life and stops his sinful habit. What will he do with these ten extra hours now? The wise thing would be to spend those hours engaged in activities that enhance spiritual life. This person could watch good Christian videos, read great Christian biographies, or study the Bible. If the ten "free hours" are not filled with something, the old devil will return.

The real problem with someone who gets victory and then backslides is that the recurring problems become worse each time around. A person who gains victory over the enemy only to fall again into the traps of familiar sins, often finds himself more out of control than before beginning his spiritual pursuit. Why? Again, Jesus made it clear. When any evil spirit, which had departed, returns and finds there is again "room for him in the inn," he goes to gather his buddies (see Mt. 12:43-45). When an evil spirit moves back into an empty heart, he brings more devils with him. Jesus said that the number of additional devils would be seven. Based on His words, we can assume that each time a person overcomes and then allows the same spirit to return, the increase in the number of devils in his life is at least 800 percent, because he now has eight devils. Now if someone who has been delivered of several demons allows them back and each one brings seven friends from the kingdom of darkness, there is a major increase of demonic power in that individual's life.

The increase mentioned above is not just in the number of spirits working against a life. The enemy also becomes stronger because the additional devils invited to move in are more wicked than the original occupant. This is what Jesus taught. An unclean spirit upon returning will bring seven devils more wicked than himself. We can now understand why a person who backslides or relapses is often submerged into worse problems than before his deliverance. If a person forms a pattern of evicting the devils only to have them return again, the power of the devil will be growing, not shrinking, in his life. It is obvious why the stronghold of the enemy becomes so great in some hearts.

There are three key words Jesus used in Matthew 12 that will help us continue with our study. They are: *empty, swept,* and *garnished.* Let's take a closer look at what these words mean. The Greek word for *empty* is *scholazo.*[1] It means to "cease from labor, to be idle and to loiter." This Greek word also means to have a place that is unoccupied. In the illustration Jesus gave, the unclean spirit had left the person. This means the laborious struggle was over, but did the person find a positive way to expend his energies or just begin to loiter? Jesus used this word to describe a heart that was no longer occupied by the devil. The evil spirit had gone and the house was empty because no one was living there. This would be like moving furniture out of a room. It means there is an unoccupied space available.

It has long been said, "an idle mind is the devil's workshop." It seems when the mind is not activated with positive spiritual things, it becomes like a storage bin waiting to be filled. When the Holy Spirit is not invited to fill a heart, there is space for the devil to return. It is vital that one who has found any degree of freedom not leave himself empty and open to the enemy. A person must take the initiative to hang a "no vacancy" sign on his heart and mind by filling the emptiness with God.

The next word we want to look at is *swept*. The Greek word for *swept* is *saroo*.[2] This word means "to sweep clean." It means the person has cleaned the house of his heart. When former occupants move out, they often leave their garbage behind. After forcing the devil to move out, you will have to sweep up his debris because residents leave a residue. *Swept* means the room has been cleared, cleaned, and is now accessible. Too many times people make themselves both available and accessible to the devil. The goal should be to be neither. It is important to get the room cleared and cleaned, there is no question about that. The purpose of custodial work within a heart is not so the "old" occupant can return, but rather so a "new" occupant can gain access. This process is like mopping and disinfecting the room.

The final word we want to look at here is *garnished*. The Greek word for *garnished* is *kosmeo*.[3] It comes from the root word *kosmos* and means "cleaned out to put into proper order." This word literally means to arrange or ornament. It has been translated in the Bible as adorn, garnish and trim. This means the house gets redecorated. Owners often do this after a renter moves out. *Garnished* means that the room has been made attractive. In the story Jesus told, the person had prepared his heart to attract a new occupant. This would be like painting the walls, putting up wallpaper and trimming the woodwork. *Garnished* means the room has been cleared, cleaned, and is now attractive.

If you are "empty, swept, and garnished" you will attract the devils back. The only way to prevent their return is to fill yourself with God. Once delivered, do not set yourself up or leave yourself open for the return of the bad boys. Don't allow it to be said of your life, "the boys are back in town." Drive them out never to return to your life again. And whatever you do, don't advertise a vacancy. Make yourself available, accessible, and attractive only to the Lord. Fill yourself up with God and there will be "no room in the inn" when the bad boys attempt to return. Do this and your "room" will have great potential!

Don't Help the Devil

The Word of the Lord gives clear instruction and a sure promise to those who resist the devil. The Scripture declares:

> *Submit yourselves therefore to God. Resist the devil, and he will flee from you. Draw nigh to God, and He will draw nigh to you. Cleanse your hands, ye sinners; and purify your hearts, ye double minded* (James 4:7-8).

We are instructed to *resist*, not *assist*, the devil. What could be more foolish than to help the devil's cause rather than to hurt his program for our lives? To illustrate this, I want to tell you about a near-tragic automobile accident in 1995. We were returning to Cincinnati, Ohio, on a Saturday from a missions meeting in Indianapolis, Indiana. The winter weather was terrible, and the interstate roads were covered with ice and snow.

My husband was driving as we started down a hill that had a bridge at the bottom of it. Seeing the bridge and knowing it would freeze before the road, he realized he was traveling too fast for the conditions and wanted to slow down. We were in a 1994 Lincoln Mark VIII. He laid his hand on the shift lever to put it into neutral. His intentions were to tap the brakes and slow the vehicle down, limiting the risk of tires sliding. This was a good plan, but he executed it poorly. He accidentally put the gear into reverse sending the car into an immediate spin. As it whirled off the road, it slid down an embankment racing us toward concrete dividers that were piled in the median for road construction. Amazingly, when I cried out the name of Jesus, the car slowed and my husband regained control. He was able to bring us back onto the roadway just in time to cross the bridge. It was a very close call—and it was scary! Johnny immediately exclaimed, "The devil tried to kill us!" It was understandable why he truly felt the enemy was out to destroy us. I, too, had been very frightened. But I had a different take on who was the responsible party. I wasn't in the mood to let my husband slide by and blame the devil so I immediately piped back to him, "Well, you helped him!" Later we laughed about this incident, but not at that moment. How often do we blame the devil for our own lack of wisdom? When we fail to execute wisdom in life, we become coworkers with satan, aiding our own demise.

You really do not need to fear the devil's attack or what he may do to you. He has limits and you have the ultimate control. He may take action against you but your reaction and where you go from there is entirely up to you. It is not what the devil is doing that should concern you. It is how you are helping him that should sound the alarm. The devil is out to kill, steal and destroy you. Make sure you don't help him!

Let me emphasize the importance of maintaining the victories you have won. God wants to give you victory that is complete and lasting—not just temporary relief. Too many people only want God, revival, or the preacher in those moments of acute agony. In reality, though, they need victory over their chronic conditions in life. We have too many "aspirin takers" only wanting temporary relief of the acute pain sin has caused them. As a pastoral caregiver for many years, I have discovered that people are looking to feel better. They are not seeking change. Feeling better is only permanent when it is associated with meaningful change.

Determine that you are going to have victory—real, lasting victory. General Douglas MacArthur proclaimed, "There is no substitute for victory." There isn't! You may win your war battle by battle, but whatever you do—win! We must learn from those who have fought for freedom. World history can also teach us much about winning battles in the spirit. When you get fed up with the bondage, you will fight. When you are really determined, you will win. No longer will a foreign power occupy your territory. Once you have gained victory, you must never again forfeit your rights to the devil.

Walking Through Dry Places

There is truth and spiritual insight contained in the specific wording Jesus used to explain what happens when a person once delivered is again defiled. In the text, He said the evil spirit "walketh through dry places" (see Mt. 12:43). Life becomes a wilderness and leaves bewilderment. The lack of moisture leaves the land barren. The heat rises and the desert creatures take over your life. Whether in the natural world or your own soul, you must have the rain from Heaven. Otherwise, you will become dry.

The devil likes it dry. When it is too dry for too long, it becomes a drought. Is this not the pattern of many denominations and professing believers? I think, yes. Most movements and denominations sprang forth from revivals, but many have failed to keep the river of God flowing. Personally we will dry up, too, unless we purposely keep the river running through our own spirit. Revivals will only sustain those who sustain them. Those who delight in the law of the Lord are like trees planted by a river. Those who walk in the counsel of the ungodly, stand in the way of sinners, or sit in the seat of the scornful live in a dry and barren land (see Ps.1). We must not resist God's will for us, His way in us, or His Word to us. When we resist God, we become rebels, and the rebellious live in a dry land (see Ps. 68:6). And in this dry land, the devil rules. He does not like the water. Is that why those pigs ran to the sea? That's a simple plan for victory—we can run to the river and drown the devils in our lives! The river of renewal will cause you to live while destroying the works of satan. This water is the water that Jesus promised to the Samaritan woman at the well.

> *Whosoever drinketh of the water that I shall give him shall never thirst; but the water that I shall give him shall be in him a well of water springing up into ever-lasting life* (John 4:14).

Jesus is the *source* and we are the *course* of the living water. It flows from Him and through us. This is clear in the statement made by Jesus in Scripture. Christ offers living water to all who are thirsty and will drink. But, it is out of our bellies that the water flows. Consider these words:

> *...If any man thirst, let him come unto Me, and drink. He that believeth on Me, as the scripture hath said, out of his belly shall flow rivers of living water* (John 7:37b-38).

This concept is often interpreted as though the living water flows out of the person who is thirsty. But this is not true. The person becomes the channel, but not the source. He or she is only the water pipe. Jesus is the water. A person filled with the Spirit has a river within him, but the river has its own power and comes from God alone. There is substantial teaching in both Old and New Testaments that speaks of a river as a symbol of the Spirit of God. There are Bible verses that tell us it is a river into which we enter, and those that teach there is a river inside us. We get into the river and the river gets into us. Oh, that we might get into the river! Oh, that the river might get into us!

Maybe you know you are dry, but feel there is no hope for rain in the forecast. No matter how dry yesterday was, you can be wet with the dew of Heaven today! The promise of receiving the Spirit is granted to those who ask. Those who are hungry will be filled and those who are thirsty will be satisfied. No matter how dry your family, church or soul, God can send a downpour into your life. It may seem like a wilderness journey, but remember it was in a desert that God supernaturally supplied water to the children of Israel. Claim the promise of God to quench your thirst and let your testimony be the same as that of the wandering Jews of long ago. "He opened the rock, and the waters gushed out; they ran in the dry places like a river" (Ps. 105:41).

Lift your voice and turn your heart to God as David did in his time of personal drought. Long for the Lord and seek after Him. Let these words define your determination to turn your desert into a rose garden:

O God, Thou art my God; early will I seek Thee: my soul thirsteth for Thee, my flesh longeth for Thee in a dry and thirsty land, where no water is (Ps. 63:1-2).

Friend, there is a river. It is a cleansing stream. It flows from deep within. Right now you can come to this water. There is a vast supply. Jesus Christ is ready to fill you!

Endnotes

1. James Strong, *Strong's Exhaustive Concordance of the Bible* (Peabody, Massachusetts: Hendrickson Publishers, n.d.), **scholazo**, (G#4980).

2. Strong, **saroo**, (G#4563).

3. Strong, **kosmeo**, (G#2885).

Chapter Seven

BLUE VELVET

Dealing With Depression

What would you say if someone asked you, "What is the color of your day?" Life comes in living color. It has various colors, shades, tints, and hues. It is not black and white, as some believe. How boring it would be to live in a world without color. Emotions are colorful as well. There are intensities of emotion, shades of feelings, and tints of responses. The colors of all emotions need expression, however, and a balance and blending of colors is also needed.

Think for a moment about the colors of emotions. What does yellow "feel" like to you? What about green? Red? Blue? What mental state does each describe? We hear about people being green with jealousy, red with anger, and blue with heartache. If blue represents sadness, how much blue should there be in life and when does blue need to change?

Many songs, poems and stories have been written about people feeling blue. One of these, "Blue Velvet," was a song by

Bobby Vinton. He sang about a woman in a blue velvet dress. While the song spoke of beauty, it also expressed the deep sorrow of seeing the blue velvet dress "through tears." Elvis Presley became the "king" of rock music as he expressed himself through exuberant music with a fervent beat. On the other hand, he knew the depths of depression and sang many songs reflecting this emotion. Many of these songs referred to the color blue. For example, "Blue Suede Shoes," "Hawaiian Blues," etc. One of his albums was called "Blue Moods." Elvis attracted thousands because his music expressed his own emotions, which were like those of the listeners. And nothing spoke more keenly of his deeply religious roots as the song "Crying in the Chapel."

Each person has a range of emotions from ecstasy to rage. Each day we have to deal with feelings and emotions, our own as well as those of people around us. Few of us know how or what to do with them. Believers experience the same spectrum of emotions because we are still human. It is very important that we understand our emotions. We can learn how to profit from each of our feelings, even our feelings of loss. The enemy likes to take these "blue" feelings and feed us his own interpretation. Ignorance is not bliss—it leaves us vulnerable and confused. Let's take a look at understanding and managing our moods.

Few of us would say that feeling great is a problem. We seem to be at home with the good times and believe they are directly from the hand of God. It is the down times or bad times we often have problems with. But in these times, too, God is still God. If we properly manage difficult times, I believe we will do much to enhance our spiritual lives and destroy satan's scheme to defeat us. Proverbs 4:7 tells us to get wisdom, but with all our getting, "get understanding." Understanding can disarm potential threats to our lives. It is my hope that by sharing these insights you will better deal with your times of distress and be able to "shrink" any potential for damage.

Moods and emotions are part of a healthy life and have their appropriate place. Emotions can range from ecstasy to the depths of despair. For each, there is a time and a season. Ecclesiastes chapter 3 frames this subject very well. There is, indeed, a time for sadness as well as a time for laughter. Life has a natural swing to it. It is like the pendulum on a clock swinging equally in each direction. It is not limited to movement on just one side. If the pendulum stops swinging, the clock will not work. Likewise, emotions must have a healthy rhythm as well. The "clock of life" is broken when the pendulum of emotional flexibility sticks to one side or quits swinging. For example, when sadness persists for an extended period, the "time" for sadness becomes "stuck." God gave human beings a wide range of emotions to enable us to respond to things, situations and other people. He created us with the ability to experience grief and sadness as well as joy and peace. A balance of these emotions must be maintained in order to have a stable life.

A Closer Look at Depression

Depression is one of the major illnesses in American society and is no respecter of age, race, or gender. It is one of the major tools satan uses against the believer. It is his tactic to get one "stuck" in depression. I say "stuck" because depression in itself is not a negative or sinful thing. Depression, in fact, is a healing emotion. God designed depression as a way for the body to replenish and restore itself physically and emotionally. Sometimes it is difficult for Christians to accept depression as a gift from God, yet the psalmist wrote that in the valley "He restoreth my soul" (see Ps. 23:3). During a period of depression it is natural to have "down time." Although unpleasant at the time, it is to be expected and profitable.

The topic of depression is addressed so little and so poorly in the Christian community that it is very often misunderstood. The lack of knowledge and understanding causes good people who are hurting to be judged unfairly. For example, some in the Christian community believe depression is a sin. If depression persists, they believe that some "hidden sin" must be present. Of course, when the "hidden sin" cannot be identified, deeper depression results from self-condemnation. Depression then becomes a vicious circle. The solution to this dilemma is the ability and willingness to understand the symptoms, causes and treatment options for the condition.

There are two major categories to be considered when discussing depression—reactive depression, and endogenous or biochemical depression. There are degrees and subtypes for both of these categories of depression. They range from "the blues" to "black despair." We all have moments of depression from time to time. It is part of the cycle of life. However, if the depression lasts for an extended period of time, it can become a "pit." It is quite common to hear people talk about feeling in "the pits." Most of the discussion in this chapter deals with "feeling in the pits" or having "the blues." It is important to mention, however, that without spiritual intervention and/or treatment, it is possible for the "the blues" to get out of hand and progress into a more serious type of depression with physiological complications. This type is referred to as clinical depression.

I have chosen not to address clinical depression that is caused by biochemical problems. I am not a professional in that field, neither do I attempt to prescribe what one should do in that situation. It is also not my intent to add to the already heavy load of those who suffer from clinical depression. However, I do believe much of the depression in our society and in the minds of believers could be changed or "shrunk" by allowing the Holy Spirit to do His work.

There are all sorts of condemning books about people who are depressed. There are also those who speak out against emotional worship or feelings being expressed to God. To hear some, you would think that feelings were evil or sinful. But there is no feeling or emotion that is sinful! What is done with the feeling or emotion is what determines its effect in our lives.

Feeling down is not a sin. Having "the blues," which is one form of depression, is certainly not a sin. But how do you know if you have "the blues"? What are some "blues clues"? What are the common roots of depression? The answers to these questions are important because people seem to be plagued daily with problems that can evolve into a vicious cycle of depression in their lives.

The Blues Clues

The signs of depression are many and include but are not limited to:

1. Moodiness or a significant change in mood such as unusual irritability or passivity

2. Changes in appetite

3. Changes in sleep patterns

4. Loss of interest in hobbies or things normally enjoyed

5. Desire for isolation

6. Loss of interest in personal appearance

7.   Preoccupation with sad thoughts or death

8.   Low energy levels, often appearing tired, lazy, lethargic, and/or unmotivated

Sometimes depression takes on the form of physical illness in the body. Of course, not every illness is a result of depression, but this is often the case. Medical doctors tell us that a large percentage of the physical illnesses from which people suffer have emotional roots. I am not saying the problems are "all in their heads" or that they are all psychosomatic. However, the causes of these physical illnesses often originate from unresolved emotional issues of the soul. These issues, when internalized, can cause serious physical illness and can, if left unattended, become life threatening. For example, stress can cause high blood pressure that leads to strokes, heart problems, etc. These problems may not be organically-based but become serious medical problems when the emotional roots remain untreated.

It is important to remember, though, that not all chronic illnesses are a result of emotions or depression. I would not want to add more to the burden of the person suffering with a chronic condition. But on the other hand, we must not overlook those who suffer physically as a result of emotional pain. If you suffer physically and the doctors do not seem to be able to locate the cause, it would be worthwhile to assess the possibility that the body is manifesting depression through physical illness.

This topic reminds me of a lady at the Arkansas camp meetings I attended. We could have written her into the program of every service. She was very depressed. Her house was a mess and she was constantly in bed sick. Her depression manifested itself physically. She would receive prayer only to have the pain change locations in her body. She never got well, but she testified that she was touched every time we prayed. If her head was hurting and we prayed for it, the headache left but her hip started hurting. So we would pray for her hip and it would be healed but her stomach would begin hurting. It seemed that God was relocating the pain within her body. The next service something else was wrong and she needed special prayer (or, more accurately for her, attention) again. It seemed as though she had "musical pain," and we could never tell in what part of her body it would stop. I personally believe this was a "spirit of infirmity" that needed to be addressed. The illness was in her spirit, not in her body. Although the manifestation was with physical symptoms, the root was depression.

Common Roots of Depression

1. Depression results from some kind of loss.

Losses may be great or small, temporary or permanent. But a loss is a loss. We will feel and grieve our losses, even if only at the subconscious level. The Bible tells us that "hope deferred maketh the heart sick" (Prov. 13:12a). This is a definite cause of depression. When what we hoped for is delayed or denied, our heart becomes sick.

Many losses that we humans suffer can manifest themselves through depression. The loss of people, property, position, and power can all lead to "the blues." It is natural to feel sadness, even overwhelming sadness, immediately following such an event. That is the way God created us. But He also gave us the ability to move on to healing. When a person cannot recover or chooses not to move beyond the loss, he or she becomes vulnerable to a more serious depression. The length of the recovery period is different for each person and is directly related to the loss experienced. In other words, the level of reaction to the loss is in direct proportion to the perceived value of the loss incurred.

For example, the death of a spouse is a significant loss and will be felt deeply for a long while. It leaves a vacancy for a lifetime. Some people think that we should "get over" the death of a loved one. While there is no way to "get over" it, there is a way to "get through" it. God will take us through these times if we allow Him to do so. We will never be as though the loss didn't occur, but life will become manageable and can even take on new meaning if we allow the Lord to direct our steps. Depression caused by a great loss is natural and will pass as the loss is processed one day at a time. The pain, although uncomfortable, is inevitable and should be considered healthy. Yes, loss and grief can change sunny skies to blue, but there is no grief so deep that the Holy Spirit cannot find us. There is no sorrow too deep for Him to heal. God is a God of comfort.

I remember when my sister, Sandy, lost her husband to an accident in 1983. She was only 29 and he was 31. They had two precious children, ages 2 and 7, at the time. That was one of the saddest days of my life and definitely their saddest. We went to Norman, Oklahoma, to be with them, and I can still recall the hours of tears and groans. There seemed to be no words to console and no salve to soothe. I will never forget the scene. Sandy was on her bed grieving so deeply that I was concerned for her physical life. Her agony filled the room like a thick cloud as family members stood helplessly around. Then we began to pray as a family and turned to the only source we knew—God.

I will never forget that evening when we lifted our voices together on behalf of a little family whose dear father had been taken suddenly. They hadn't even had the time to say "goodbye." It seemed as though a world of grief had been poured into the air. But prayers were being lifted. Our voices blended and our hearts united while asking for the only comfort we knew. Suddenly a language we did not understand but had heard many times began to roll over Sandy's lips. The power of the Holy Spirit filled the room dispersing the cloud of grief. Then the peace of God flooded our hearts and our prayers were suddenly spoken in the tongues of angels. The sweet Comforter had come, and the comfort that we so earnestly sought was found.

I had known the comfort of the Holy Spirit all my life but it was never more vivid than on that day. That was the first of many experiences my sister would have as God held the hand of a widow and fathered a family through grief. Even in deep sorrow, God is more than enough.

The same feelings associated with grief and loss occur with the loss of a job or any other form of security. Fear creeps in and increases our unpleasant feelings. It is easy to become defensive and turn the feelings associated with these losses into bitterness and contempt. Blaming ourselves, others, or even God allows these losses to destroy the vision for our future. It also prevents our own desire to be well. Do you remember Jesus' asking the man at Bethesda's pool, "Wilt thou be made whole?" (Jn. 5:6) That is the only question that matters. Do you want to be well? If so, victory will come to you as you pursue the presence of God.

It is very appropriate and natural to feel the pain of a loss, but we don't need to stop living. It is imperative to do whatever is necessary to re-establish personal focus. Then God will come and direct our steps and restore our soul as He promised. Allowing these issues to go unresolved creates the risk of depression "settling in" and taking residence. Sometimes depression even becomes a "friend" in our loss, because it is all that is left of the experience we had. How easy it is to hold on to depression and fail to work through the stages of grief. God has answers for us in these times of life, but we must want them. He will not force us to be healed or restored.

There is an old saying that says, "Time heals all." But the reality is that while time diminishes the intensity of the loss, only Christ can heal. He did not come just to redeem us from hell. He also came that life would be abundant here on earth and eternal in the world to come (see Jn. 10:10).

2.   Depression comes from physical exhaustion.

In Chapter Two of this book I shared my own experience with depression. A major factor in my "blue journey" was physical exhaustion. This physical condition was the result of my having maintained poor boundaries. Boundaries protect individual limits and respect "personal space." It may take saying "no" to a few requests that people ask of you. But you must understand that you don't have the time or energy to do everything. You may need to ask your children to do their own laundry or set a bedtime for the household. Physical energy depletion puts your body under stress (or distress) and it eventually begins to break down. When this happens, there are numerous physical and emotional symptoms that can occur. It is important to give your body the rest it needs before it burns out. This can keep clinical depression along with physiological complications from becoming manifest.

I believe many failures of great people of God have been born out of exhaustion. Depleting our bodies leaves us feeling low. To avoid this feeling of depression many people have resorted to fulfilling sinful lust. This creates an adrenaline rush and temporarily replaces the depression with a false high. Of course, this rush is gone in a matter of minutes, adding guilt and shame to the depression. What a combination! The end result of this cycle is very destructive to the individual and to those around him. This person's sense of self-worth is then calculated by the degree that his failure hurts the Kingdom of God. The consequences of falling from grace are obvious, but often the causes are misunderstood. To avoid failing in this area we need to understand and manage our physical bodies and emotions (soul) with wisdom (spirit).

3. Depression results from disappointment with God.

A common root of depression for the Christian is disappointment with God. Most people have personal expectations about what God should do for them. Much of this disappointment comes from a distorted theology caused by taking Scripture out of its original context. After all, if God cannot "fix" it, then it is hopeless, right? This irrational belief system leads to confusion and discouragement. Because the Christian is often interested in "protecting God's reputation," these intense feelings of disappointment are buried, only to erupt later in the form of anger or depression.

Most of us at one time or another have questioned why God did not seem to "come through" for us. Mary must have felt very confused at the cross. After all, she had been chosen to be the mother of the Messiah. The scene before her at the cross was not what she envisioned the day the angel appeared and gave her the "good news." Our interpretation of what we believe God said can also create confusion. It is often difficult to see the whole picture and there are times when the "Footprints" poem on the refrigerator will just not suffice. We need understanding and patience to "wait it out" and "hang on" to our faith during difficult situations.

The Bottom Line About Depression

It is important to notice that the roots of depression can originate from physical, emotional or spiritual stressors. It can even be a combination of all three. Because the coping skills and defense mechanisms of the body are weak or broken down, depression often results in feelings of hopelessness and powerlessness. People who are depressed need rest and refreshing. Everyone walks through valleys. But the objective is to do just that—walk through! They must walk through, not live (or die) in the valley!

Even in the valley of the shadow of death, there is hope. We do not have to fear. No matter what the situation, we must never give up hope. We can be happy again, but we must regain genuine hope. It doesn't matter what shade of blue your circumstance is, there is hope in the Lord.

Praise ye the Lord. Praise the Lord, O my soul. While I live will I praise the Lord: I will sing praises unto my God while I have any being. Put not your trust in princes, nor in the son of man, in whom there is no help. His breath goeth forth, he returneth to his earth; in that very day his thoughts perish. Happy is he that hath the God of Jacob for his help, whose hope is in the Lord his God: Which made Heaven, and earth, the sea, and all that therein is: which keepeth truth for ever: which executeth judgment for the oppressed: which giveth food to the hungry. The Lord looseth the prisoners: the Lord openeth the eyes of the blind: the Lord raiseth them that are bowed down: the Lord loveth the righteous: the Lord preserveth the strangers; He relieveth the fatherless and widow: but the way of the wicked He turneth upside down. The Lord shall reign for ever, even thy God, O Zion, unto all generations. Praise ye the Lord (Psalms 146).

Chapter Eight

Changing Colors

God's Plan for Deliverance

Once we find ourselves in a pit of despair or depression, it is very easy to stay there. It's as though we want to wallow in our problems and consider ourselves a victim, almost to the point that we take no action to aid our own recovery. But I am the only one who can paint the color of my world. The goal of counselors and teachers should be to help us "help ourselves." Those people in the counseling field who try to tell us that they can resolve our depression are deceiving us and deceiving themselves. The real solution is for each of us to learn skills and insights in order to "recover ourselves." This principle is taught in the Scriptures. We must each do everything we can, then trust God to do the rest. This is such a critical point that I want to look again at the following Scripture:

> *...instructing those that oppose themselves; if God per-adventure will give them repentance to the acknowledging of the truth; and that they may recover*

themselves out of the snare of the devil, who are taken captive by him at his will (2 Timothy 2:25-26).

Solutions

So what do we need to do to recover and get out of the snare of the devil? Where is our "help"? We are prone to look outside ourselves for deliverance. But in a very real sense, our help will come from within our own hearts. God is our ultimate help. Real deliverance comes from Him. But we must want Him and seek after Him. It is our faith in His Word that will ultimately bring relief from "the blues." How? The Bible says that the Word of God is sharper than any two-edged sword and separates the soul and the spirit (see Heb. 4:12). In a practical application, that means the Word of God will separate the soul (issues of the emotions, attitudes, will, and thinking) from the spirit (God-connection).

Depression must come under subjection to the Word. Even in depression it is possible to maintain spiritual sharpness when the Word of God is applied. It is faith in His Word that will ultimately dilute a drab blue to bring a radiant hue. That's why we need to read the Word and seek after the Lord. The Scriptures admonish us to "Call upon Me in the day of trouble; I will deliver thee..." (Ps. 50:15).

Many great patriarchs of the Bible, including Moses, Elijah, David and Job, experienced depression and found their solution in the Lord. John the Baptist asked if Jesus was the Christ when he was in a dark dungeon awaiting execution. John knew Jesus was the Christ! He knew it in his spirit. The first time he had ever seen Jesus he proclaimed He was the Lamb of God. (See John 1:29.) So what had happened? John was in prison and he was doubtful and afraid. What did Christ offer this man at that moment of inquiry? He told him only of the miraculous things that were happening and left it to John to decide.

Where you now live may seem like prison, but you can still think. So, what do you think? Who do you think Jesus is? What do you think you should do? You must receive Him by faith and take proactive steps to walk out of your prison of depression, addiction, or whatever name is on your dungeon. He will be there with you!

The Book of Psalms is very colorful and has a lot of "blue" in it. We read songs written about David's depression and God's deliverance. David suffered tremendous loss. He lost moral character, friendships, a child, loyalty, rest, hope, and a dream. Yet in all his failures and disappointments we find King David continually turning to God. Despite his losses, he was a "man after God's own heart" (see 1 Sam. 13:14; 16:12; Acts 13:22). Why? Because he sought a genuine relationship with God. David did a lot of praying and a lot of singing. Both are helpful in overcoming "the blues." David had a unique ability to keep moving when he was depressed. Watch him "walk through" his valley. Somehow he always found a lily or a stone or something of value in the valley to kill his giant or restore his soul.

Tell Yourself The Truth

If you are to have victory over depression you will have to get honest with yourself. You will have to start telling yourself and others the truth. Too often we live in denial or do not face reality. Here are some keys to unlock the prisons of depression.

1.   Admit you are depressed.

Deliverance from anything begins with acknowledgment. Admit to God that you are depressed. He knows it anyway. He won't be upset or angry with you. Take the time to count your losses and acknowledge the feelings associated with those losses.

To deny those feelings delays the process of healing. We have a Christ that is touched and moved by the feelings of our infirmities (see Heb. 4:15). Until we are able to acknowledge and feel our infirmities and pain, we cannot identify with Christ. Likewise, until we acknowledge and feel our pain, we do not allow Him to identify with us. Our greatest tendency is to deny, but God calls upon us to acknowledge.

2.   Acknowledge to God your desire to be delivered.

He knows what is needed before you ask, but He tells you that you need to ask anyway. Why? Because you will benefit from hearing yourself admit aloud your need. God always respects honesty. We tend to skirt issues when we are uncomfortable and talk to God only about the good times. He calls upon us to ask.

3.   Acknowledge your need for healing to others.

Acknowledge your need for healing to others by enlisting the prayers of those in whom you have confidence. Make an open statement of your desire to be whole. Scripture tells us to confess our faults (sin or offense) one to another and to pray one for another that we may be healed (see Jas. 5:16). This principle is helpful in matters of sin as well as pain.

4.   Accept nothing less than victory.

Determine in your heart that you are going to find a solution to your need. The woman with the issue of blood determined to press through the crowd to touch Jesus (see Mt. 9:20-21). You, too, can determine to find a solution. You can press through whatever is standing between you and your victory.

Resolutions

Let's get down to the "nitty-gritty" of developing your devil shrinking skills! How can you shrink the devil of depression?

(Again, I am dealing with depression that does not have a bio-chemical root. The depression I am referring to originates from poor choices, experienced losses, or from your own efforts to manipulate others.) To shrink the depression devil you must have a very clear resolve. You must purpose in your heart to stop the cycle of depression.

1.   RESOLVE to stop the cycle of depression.

Get up, get out and get going! In other words, put some action into the equation. There may be days when you will not feel like "getting out," but don't allow these feelings to dictate your behavior. Moving beyond feelings is not the same as deny-ing them. Getting past "the blues" is setting feelings aside for a time and taking positive action toward recovery. Sometimes great effort is needed to get beyond feelings, but it is possible to overcome them. Push a little, rest a little, push more, rest a little and move on. Exercise caution and know your limits, but don't be afraid to give an extra push from time to time. Step out and step over your problem!

Understand that gloom is not a friend and that things done to reinforce it are destroying the abundant life available to you. Excuses are only a method of prolonging "the blues." Only you can give a gigantic tug and let God help you get up and out! One thing is certain, taking no action to relieve depression means misery and ineffective living. The four lepers in the Old Testament had a choice. If they sat at the entrance of the gate, they knew they would die. But if they went into the city, they knew they would die there of famine. They chose to die on the move (see 2 Kings 7:3-4). When they took a risk and moved, God moved for them. You will find that when you take one step, God will take two. God is on your side and He will come through for you, but you must take a step in the right direction. Get up and move. A moving target is always more difficult to hit. Tell the devil that if he wants to attack you, he will have to aim at a moving target. Don't sit there and die!

2.   RESOLVE to change thought patterns.

Too much negative thinking is depressing in itself. Most of these thoughts are probably self-focused anyway and need to be diminished. Limit the time you dwell on these issues. If you have to set aside a time to worry and fret, do so. When that time is over, *stop it!* The psalmist said that "weeping may endure for a night, but joy cometh in the morning" (Ps. 30:5b). Limit the weeping; tap into the joy!

3.   RESOLVE to stop the pity party.

Stop feeling sorry for yourself. Ask yourself, "If tomorrow they were to begin killing sick people, would I be sick?" You might be surprised at your answer. When the Nazis were killing sick people in concentration camps, there were not many grumbling people. They dragged their bodies out of bed and worked in pitiful conditions because they understood that to be sick was to be dead. It isn't much different today. Real life depends on your deciding to live it!

I have had to overcome tremendous problems with my hands. Surgeries and other procedures have left me handicapped for long periods of time. Even after permanent damage I came to realize that I am more than hands. I can contribute in spite of my problem. When this physical body is decayed, "I" live. You are more than a body; you are more than your "blues." Shrink the debilitating circumstances of your life and get on with it! God will meet you at the point of your need. He loves you dearly and wants you to have joy. One enemy of your joy is self-pity. Look around to find someone less fortunate and become grateful again. Give your life meaning by giving yourself to God and those around you. Quit limiting yourself to body problems, family traits, or other roadblocks. You are more than a body. You are part of a family, but still more than a family member. You are a living soul with untapped potential. Don't feel sorry for yourself. Instead, see yourself as God sees you. Jeremiah 1:5 speaks of God's plans for you before conception. What did God create you to be? Find out, and with His help, become it. John 1:12 teaches us that we are given power to become the sons of God. There is no time or room for a pity party. Stop the pity and start the party. Start becoming who God created you to be.

4.   RESOLVE not to play the blame game.

It is imperative that you refuse to become bitter. Do you want an excuse to remain depressed or do you want to be whole? Joseph found himself in a pit but he didn't decorate it. His brothers put him there but God moved one of them to get him out (see Gen. 37). Your gloom doesn't have to be your tomb. Joseph was betrayed but he didn't use that as an excuse. He became useful and in the end, he won. He was lied about. He was forgotten. He was kept in a dungeon for two years, but he still welcomed the opportunity to provide for the needs of his jealous family. Satan meant it for evil. He intended to have a "heyday" with Joseph's situation. But God took a terrible situation and used it for good. Who shrunk and who grew in this situation? God grew and satan shrunk!

It is important to remember that what others do to you is not your responsibility, but how you respond is. God will give you enough grace to deal with any situation if you will only receive it. As the Scriptures teach, He will not allow you to be tempted above what you are able to bear, but will make a way if you trust Him (see 1 Cor. 10:13). When we let all things work together for good, we will learn the greatest lesson in life—that all the situations we go through are for the purpose of conforming us to the image of God (see Rom. 8:28-29). Get good out of everything. Don't waste any trial. Grow where you are. Glean from all of life's lessons.

Let me say at the conclusion of this chapter that clinical depression, a depression with biochemical roots or physiological complications, is treatable. Never give up hope; instead pursue physical, emotional, and spiritual health. God is faithful and His love reaches out in the midst of your deepest depression. He will sustain you and hold you until the storm has passed and you are on your feet again.

Anything that interferes with your ability to enjoy life needs attention. Anything that hinders your effectiveness for God deserves your focus. My prayer for you is that God will give you the patience, endurance, courage and wisdom to find your way to sunshine. There you can exchange your ashes for beauty and receive the joy of the Lord for your mourning. Take the necessary steps to remove "the blues" from your life and develop patience, persistence, and character in the process.

Nelson Mandela was put into prison but he never became a prisoner. He always had a regal "air" about him. He chose forgiveness for his oppressors. He did not become depressed. Mandela viewed his oppressors as the ones who were oppressed. He remained optimistic and free on the inside. Yes, even prison is not an excuse for long-term "blues." It is a choice you must make. What color will your life be? You cannot always choose your circumstances but you can choose your colors.

Now the God of peace, that brought again from the dead our Lord Jesus, that great shepherd of the sheep, through the blood of the everlasting covenant, make you perfect in every good work to do His will, working in you that which is wellpleasing in His sight, through Jesus Christ; to whom be glory for ever and ever. Amen (Hebrews 13:20-21).

Chapter Nine

The Magnificent Seven

Weapons of Christian Warfare

Recently I was talking with one of my dear friends in the ministry, Lila Terhune. Lila's husband, Bob, was in the movie industry for 40 years. He was a stunt man and had doubled for many well-known actors, including John Wayne. He was in the movie *The Magnificent Seven*. I had already determined that the focus of the latter part of this book was to be on the magnificence of God and not on the schemes of satan. When telling my friend about the outline of the chapters, she said, "Why don't you write a chapter on 'The Magnificent Seven'?" Those words caused a stir inside of me. The more I meditated upon this chapter, the more I knew I wanted it to be called "The Magnificent Seven."

Before we approach the list of Seven Magnificent Weapons of Christian Warfare, let's take a brief look at the Source of our weaponry. Our God has so many attributes that it is no wonder we stand in awe of Him. These attributes are the foundation of our spiritual authority. God must be who He is so that we can do what He said we could. We engage in a battle of two conflicting worlds. In the future, when the enemy is finally destroyed, the kingdoms of this world will become the Kingdoms of our God and of His Christ and He shall reign forever and ever. Hallelujah! The purpose of the war satan has declared is to try to dethrone God. But the conclusion will come when God utterly defeats His enemies. Now, let's look closer at the God for whom we fight.

Awesome Attributes of God

Self-Existence—He is Life and the Creator of all things living. He has always existed and will never cease to be. He is the Source of all life and can recreate it as easily as He created it. He Himself was not created, for He is self-existent.

Holiness—He alone is absolutely holy. He is holy within and without. There is no inherent evil or intent of evil, for He is holy.

Benevolence—He is a gracious, loving God, always desiring and doing good. His plans and purposes are for our benefit. He is working on behalf of our best interest. He loves us, because He is Love! He does no harm, for He is benevolent.

Faithfulness—Generation to generation, He remains the same. He does exactly what He said He would do. He is not inconsistent; He is faithful.

The God to whom we surrender can be trusted. He is a holy, loving, and faithful God. Worship is not a chore or a difficult task when we consider His greatness. Comprehending God to a greater degree helps us generate meaningful worship. His character is the foundation of our faith. God certainly is not limited in the greatness of these attributes, nor is He limited in the diversity of His arsenal of weapons. With this in mind, let's now explore seven of the magnificent weapons God has given to overcome opposition and oppression of the enemy. These will serve as powerful keys to assist you in your walk with the Lord and battle with the enemy.

> *Though we walk in the flesh, we do not war after the flesh: (For the weapons of our warfare are not carnal, but mighty through God to the pulling down of strong holds;) casting down imaginations, and every high thing that exalteth itself against the knowledge of God, and bringing into captivity every thought to the obedience of Christ* (2 Corinthians 10:3-5).

Seven Magnificent Weapons of Christian Warfare

1. *The Power of Jesus*

Jesus Christ has already won our victory over the devil. The following four principles give us the power we have in Him.

- The deity of Christ

Jesus is the God man. Perfect God and perfect man. As a man He could hunger, but as God He could feed the multitude. As a man He could grow weary, but as God He could offer rest. As a man He announced, "I thirst," but as God He could say, "If any man thirst, let him come unto Me and drink" (Jn. 7:37b). Jesus was God manifest in the flesh and He has been given all power in Heaven and in earth!

- The blood of Jesus

The greatest defeat to the kingdom of darkness came through the blood of Jesus Christ. His blood satisfied the justice of God. The blood of Jesus washed away our sins, so they will be remembered against us no more. "He hath made him to be sin for us, who knew no sin; that we might be made the righteousness of God in Him" (2 Cor. 5:21). When the enemy tries to magnify your sin, magnify Christ! He cleanses and forgives our sins. When satan reminds you of your past, remind him of his future. The precious blood of Jesus fills the wonderful sea of forgetfulness.

- The resurrection of Jesus

Christ is alive. The greatest proclamation ever made was the one an angel announced to Mary on the first day of the week after Jesus' crucifixion, "He is not here, He is risen!" (see Mt. 28:6) Because He lives, we can live also. Without the resurrection we would have no hope. Had death held Him, we would still be in our sins and have no real power over our enemy. The blood of Jesus Christ coupled with His bodily resurrection gives us victory over the devil. He has died, but He rose again. Today He is not a baby in a manger or a bleeding and bruised outcast of society. He is a risen Lord who ascended in power and will return in great glory!

- The name of Jesus

Jesus is the name above all names. He was the Son of God who gave His life's blood for us and then afterward rose from the grave. Because of this sequence of events, the very mention of His name brings into any circumstance the reality of His deity, His blood and His resurrection. There is no other human name like the name of Jesus.

> God also hath highly exalted Him, and given Him a name which is above every name: that at the name of Jesus every knee should bow, of things in Heaven, and things in earth, and things under the earth; and that every tongue should confess that Jesus Christ is Lord, to the glory of God the Father (Phillipians 2:9-11).

The angel Michael and satan, while disputing over the body of Moses, were at a deadlock until Michael spoke powerful words. Michael would not use his own name, but rather said, "Satan, the Lord rebuke thee." This confrontation, recorded in the Book of Jude, gives us powerful instructions. When we are up against a wall, we must speak His name! JESUS!

2. *The Power of God's Word*

The second of the Seven Magnificent Weapons of Christian Warfare is God's Word. Let's look at what happened when Jesus Himself was confronted by the devil. Reading Matthew chapter 4 we discover that when Jesus was tempted, He quoted Scripture. The Word of God has power. Jesus is the Word that became flesh. It is imperative that we know what is written. Jesus said, "It is written" and "It is written again." We must know the Word of God and use it in our fight against sin and evil. If we want the devil to flee we must be able to invoke the Word. After Christ quoted the Word, the devils departed and angels came in their place. I would say, "The devil shrunk." Yes, the devil ran from the power of the Word and Christ's refusal to yield to his temptation.

Friend, if you want to get rid of those tormenting temptations, fill your heart with the Word of God. The Word of God is the will of God. It reveals Christ and exposes satan. It unfolds truth and exposes sin. It gives hope to the saint and warning to the sinner. It is a lamp unto your feet and a light to your path (see Ps. 119:105). It will keep you from sin and give power over satan. The Word of God is the revealed mind of Christ. Having the mind of Christ gives perfect peace. To have the mind of Christ in you, the Word of God must be in your heart. Know, obey, and speak it forth into every situation you encounter.

Above all, taking the shield of faith, wherewith ye shall be able to quench all the fiery darts of the wicked. And take the helmet of salvation, and the sword of the Spir-it, which is the word of God (Ephesians 6:16-17).

3. The Power of the Holy Spirit .

The Holy Spirit is the third magnificent weapon in our arsenal. The Spirit of God moved on the face of the waters as the opening act of creation. He hovered over the chaotic world and the earth was born. The same Spirit of God overshadowed young Mary, a virgin, and Christ was born. He rushed into the upper room and the Church was born. The Holy Spirit gives us the enablement to serve in His Kingdom and the empowerment to overcome every obstacle. Through the power of the Spirit we can crush the devil. After Christ resisted the devil in His wilderness temptation, the Bible declares He went forth "in the power of the Spirit" (see Lk. 4:14). He was able to emerge from His time of testing because he was led by the Spirit. We must be "...endued with power from on high" (Lk. 24:49). It is not our own might or power, but rather His Spirit that turns the battle in our favor. We must let the Spirit choose our battles and win our victories. "This is the word of the Lord unto Zerubbabel, saying, Not by might, nor by power, but by My Spirit, saith the Lord of hosts" (Zech. 4:6).

4. The Power of Prayer

The fourth magnificent weapon in our arsenal is prayer. When we truly understand what Jesus said about prayer and the reality of His promise, we will win our battles on our knees. Christ told his disciples:

"Verily I say unto you, If ye have faith, and doubt not, ye shall not only do this which is done to the fig tree, but also if ye shall say unto this mountain, Be thou removed, and be thou cast into the sea; it shall be done.

And all things, whatsoever ye shall ask in prayer, believing, ye shall receive" (Matthew 21:21-22).

When the people in the early Church prayed, the place around them was shaken (see Acts 4:31). The Church still has the power to shake things today, but we must pray. This is an art developed by doing it, not just reading or hearing about it. Too often, an hour is spent teaching about prayer and only minutes are given to praying. Prayer is the weapon that wins the war in the heavenlies. Prayer in the Holy Spirit is our greatest weapon. It is heavenly intelligence and has the potential of unscrambling satan's code and defeating his purposes.

Fervent, believing prayer defeats essential resources of the enemy. After the air war, ground troops can advance. We have seen this tactic used during recent conflicts in the Middle East, Europe, etc. As for the spiritual war, too many of our ground troops of service and evangelism die because we have not first won our air wars through prayer. Prayer must be a personal priority. When men and women call upon God in the name of Jesus, He answers. There is no answer like a God answer!

5. *The Power of Fasting*

Fasting is yet another of the weapons God makes available to us. The early disciples were taught a timeless truth about fasting through failure. The story is recorded in Matthew 17:14-21. A man came to Jesus concerned because the disciples could not cast a demon out of his child. Jesus delivered the young boy. The disciples then asked why they could not do it. Jesus said, "This kind comes out only by fasting and prayer!" Fasting puts greater strength into prayer.

Fasting is when a person denies himself food or drink for the explicit purpose of seeking God. It is more than just not eating. It means a person is dedicating time to God and denying self. There are many kinds of fasting illustrated in the Scriptures. "Daniel" fasts limit the types of food eaten. "Water-only" fasts and "total fasts" take nothing into the body for nourishment. Fasting, although it needs to be done wisely, is a weapon that will crucify your flesh and resurrect the life of Jesus in you.

6. The Power of Worship

Genuine worship of the true and living God is one of the greatest weapons we have. We get "in the devil's face" when we worship Jesus. Satan can't stand when we worship because he desires to receive the worship that belongs to God. He wants to be like God and receive His glory. This was his problem in the beginning.

> Again, the devil taketh Him [Jesus] up into an exceeding high mountain, and showeth Him all the kingdoms of the world, and the glory of them; and saith unto Him, All these things will I give Thee, if Thou wilt fall down and worship me. Then saith Jesus unto him, Get thee hence, satan: for it is written, Thou shalt worship the Lord thy God, and Him only shalt thou serve. Then the devil leaveth Him, and, behold, angels came and ministered unto Him (Matthew 4:8-11).

When we worship God we humiliate the devil. Think of how humiliated the devil must have become in the story of his attack on Job. Satan was trying to make a point with God. If he could not get Job to worship him, at least he wanted to get him to stop worshiping God. He went as far as God would let him, even taking the lives of Job's children. Can you imagine the humiliation satan felt when he witnessed Job's response to the news that his children had died in a disaster?

*While he was yet speaking, there came also another,
and said, Thy sons and thy daughters were eating and
drinking wine in their eldest brother's house: and,
behold, there came a great wind from the wilderness,
and smote the four corners of the house, and it fell upon
the young men, and they are dead; and I only am
escaped alone to tell thee. Then Job arose, and rent his
mantle, and shaved his head, and fell down upon the
ground, and worshipped, and said, Naked came I out
of my mother's womb, and naked shall I return thither:
the Lord gave, and the Lord hath taken away; blessed
be the name of the Lord* (Job 1:18-21).

Lifting Jesus up puts everything else underneath Him.
The enemy is subdued when God is given true worship. In the
Old Testament, 2 Chronicles 20:22, we see what happened to
the enemy when Israel worshiped. When the people of God
began to sing and praise the Lord, He ambushed their enemy.
When we praise God, God fights. We can either fight or worship. Worship is my weapon of choice.

During one of my own times of being attacked, the Holy
Spirit prompted me that we must worship in proportion to the
level of attack against us. If the attack is severe our worship
must be fervent. Remember, satan wants to stop us from worshiping God. If our worship increases with his attack, it makes
it counterproductive for him to fight against us. If the devil
takes a beating every time he comes after us, he will think
twice before he engages.

Our primary purpose of worship is to glorify God. He is worthy of our praise and worthy of our honor. Our worship reflects
our value system. God deserves to be worshiped with our time,
our energy and our money. We spend time, energy and money
on things we value. Both the Old and New Testaments speak of

these important elements in regard to our spiritual life. Our priorities are often more obvious to others than to ourselves. Do our neighbors know that worshiping God is our real priority? Is it obvious in the ways we use our time, expend energy, and spend money?

7. The Power of Forgiveness

The seventh weapon of warfare is forgiveness. The Lord's prayer teaches us that we need to forgive daily. It teaches that our own forgiveness from God is contingent upon our forgiving others. God's forgiveness to us and our forgiveness toward others frees us from bondage and positions us to resist the devil. Submit to God and resist the devil. When we become bitter, the devil has won a victory. He loves to see us resist the grace of God. God gives grace to us for anything and everything we go through. But if we fail to accept that grace, a seed of bitterness is planted in our soul. Once it takes root in our heart, it starts growing. The fruit it produces brings hurt not only to us but also to others around us. Consider the powerful insight the apostle Paul gave on this subject:

> *Follow peace with all men, and holiness, without which no man shall see the Lord: Looking diligently lest any man fail of the grace of God; lest any root of bitterness springing up trouble you, and thereby many be defiled* (Hebrews 12:14-15).

Jesus Christ gave us the perfect example of whipping the devil when He chose to forgive the very ones who crucified Him. He asked the Father to forgive them. He did not wait until His resurrection to intercede for them. That would have been much easier. It would be easier to forgive our enemies after we have overcome them. But Jesus forgave them during the moments He was hanging on the cross. He had not yet died, let alone been resurrected. He was in agony! He is our example. Young

Stephen, who was stoned for preaching the truth, followed the example well. The Book of Acts records:

> *When they heard these things, they were cut to the heart, and they gnashed on him with their teeth. But he, being full of the Holy Ghost, looked up stedfastly into heaven, and saw the glory of God, and Jesus standing on the right hand of God, and said, Behold, I see the heavens opened, and the Son of man standing on the right hand of God. Then they cried out with a loud voice, and stopped their ears, and ran upon him with one accord, and cast him out of the city, and stoned him: and the witnesses laid down their clothes at a young man's feet, whose name was Saul. And they stoned Stephen, calling upon God, and saying, Lord Jesus, receive my spirit. And he kneeled down, and cried with a loud voice, Lord, lay not this sin to their charge. And when he had said this, he fell asleep [died]* (Acts 7:54-60).

If you really want to conquer your enemies, forgive them. If you really want to defeat the devil, return good for evil. You can be sure Jesus did not tell you to "love your enemies" and "pray for your enemies" because He was being soft on the devil. Nor did He want cowards for followers. Jesus knew that the power of love and forgiveness would destroy the work of satan in your life and defeat his plan to consume you in bitterness. When difficult things happen or someone does you wrong, do not get bitter, get better! Forgive! There is no greater motivation to forgive others than knowing you have needed and received forgiveness. If you realize and value God's mercy in your own life, you will find it easier to forgive others.

Summary

Yes, you do have an enemy and there is a war raging. But victory is yours through Jesus Christ! I greatly desire that this book will help you undo many of the ropes that now bind you. I pray the chains of any oppression you have experienced will be broken and removed forever. I trust you can find full recovery and restoration from any wounds of your past. I want you to win! God wants you to win! Do you want to win? If so, keep "The Magnificent Seven" weapons ready. Use them to defeat and shrink your enemy!

Chapter Ten

These Boots Are Made for Walking

Destroying the Works of the Devil

Jesus Christ came to destroy the works of the devil (see 1 Jn. 3:8). He did not come to debate, to wound, to bargain or to confront. He came to destroy. In fact, the Scripture says the anointing destroys the yoke (see Is. 10:27). It should be no surprise, then, for Jesus Christ to be the One who destroys the devil. The name *Christ* literally means "the Anointed One." Jesus has been given all power in Heaven and in earth, including power over the devil.

So why do we tiptoe over what satan is doing? We become passive about the destruction and devastation he wreaks in our families. We become complacent to sin in our community and the people he ensnares. We just look over the moral wreck he has made of our nation and recline to watch sports or monitor stocks. We close our ears to the cries of the people of the world held captive by his chains. We take a defeatist mentality and give up, assuming we are not able to make a difference. This is called apathy! Apathy never fought a battle, much less won a war. Apathy never made it up a hill to enjoy the wind blowing against his face riding down the other side. Apathy lives a very dull life.

Instead of apathy we need action. It is time we get to "devil stompin' "! We no longer need to step around the enemy. We need to tromp on him. We need to get taps put onto our toes and spikes put onto our heels so we can make an impression on the devil. "Devil stompin' " is a learned art and it is never too late to learn. Get your boots on and dance "The Devil Stomp." This is a godly dance that is as old as the human race. It was first introduced in the garden of Eden.

> *And the Lord God said unto the serpent, Because thou hast done this, thou art cursed above all cattle, and above every beast of the field; upon thy belly shalt thou go, and dust shalt thou eat all the days of thy life: and I will put enmity between thee and the woman, and between thy seed and her seed; It shall bruise thy head, and thou shalt bruise His heel* (Genesis 3:14-15).

Genesis 3:15 is a "protoevangelum" of the Bible, meaning it is a first mention of a coming Redeemer. It foretells what the devil would do to Jesus. We think of it as a crucifixion, but the resurrection made it no more than a bruise on the heel of His foot. Yes, satan would bruise the heel of the Lord, but Christ would stomp the head of satan. Jesus stomped him good on Golgotha, but the devil has a final head "stompin' " to endure. Christ is going to tread the winepress of the fierceness and wrath of the Almighty.

> *For He must reign, till He hath put all enemies under His feet. The last enemy that shall be destroyed is death. For He hath put all things under His feet* (1 Corinthians 15:25-27a).

Under Our Feet

Even now we have power to tread on the enemy. Jesus made that promise in Luke 10:19. If we want to leave a message for the devil, we should write it on the soles of our shoes. The Scriptures teach that all things are under Jesus' feet. We are His body and all things are under His feet, so they are under our feet, too. I wonder why we stand still knowing satan is under our feet? I say, "Stomp! Dance! Dig in your heels!"

You see, our feet are a very important part of warfare. We have been shod with the preparation of the gospel of peace. They are our instruments to bring peace to this world. The children of Israel walked out of Egypt and into Canaan. Like them, we claim our territory by walking around the boundaries. Our own Jericho falls after we have marched around it. Jesus said, "Go into all the world." How will we go? We will march through the land! I wonder what we would possess if we would just get up and start walking?

Some people think everything about their lives is sovereign. They feel there is never any need to do anything because God is in control and He will do it for them. When God spoke to Abraham in Genesis 15:5, He promised him descendants. To illustrate the promise and the potential of Abraham's seed, God showed him the stars. Yes, some things are from Heaven and that should be the point of our gaze. For some things we look up. However, there are other things in our earthly habitation that depend on our efforts. When God told Abraham that He would give him the land, He gave him more to do than just look.

The Lord said unto Abram, after that Lot was separated from him, Lift up now thine eyes, and look from the place where thou art northward, and southward, and eastward, and westward: for all the land which thou seest, to thee will I give it, and to thy seed for ever. And

HONEY, I SHRUNK THE DEVIL!

I will make thy seed as the dust of the earth: so that if a man can number the dust of the earth, then shall thy seed also be numbered. Arise, walk through the land in the length of it and in the breadth of it; for I will give it unto thee (Genesis 13:14-17).

Years ago, Nancy Sinatra sang a song that said, "These boots are made for walking...and one of these days these boots are gonna walk all over you." She was speaking of a bad love relationship, but I prefer those lyrics when I think of the devil. They became powerful words to me for this message. When delivering the sermon, "Honey, I Shrunk the devil," at a women's conference held at the Brownsville Assembly of God in Pensacola, Florida, I illustrated this concept. I brought my western boots with me along with some other props and assistants to illustrate how to watch the devil shrink. I arranged for a tall man dressed like the devil to come out on the stage early in my sermon. I arranged for an adolescent, dressed identically, to come out in front of the conference participants in the middle of the sermon. Then near the end of the message, I reached into the pulpit and pulled out my boots. I asked the crowd, "What are these for?" Seemingly with one voice, they shouted back to me, "These boots are made for walking!"

Next I referenced the Bible passage where satan was cast into the bottomless pit (see Rev. 20). I said I would like to go to the edge of the pit just before they "shut him up." I would like to peer over the edge and call down and say, "Devil, you have had your day and now I am going to walk all over you!" With that I put on my boots, pulled out a plastic devil doll dressed just like the bigger devils and began to stomp. Later, I brought out numerous little devil dolls and began to throw them into the audience. Women were throwing them on the floor and stomping them. The dolls were thrown from person to person until they were torn apart—an arm here and a leg there. We had a wonderful time of "devil stompin' "!

That experience was more than a bunch of women showing emotion. It was symbolic of the determination each one had to stomp the devil that had "been messin' where he should not have been messin' "! I know in reality that display did not crush satan, but it was quite therapeutic to use our energies in agreement with the idea of stomping the enemy. Sometimes it is good to put your energy into what you are doing mentally. If the enemy is "under our feet" then why not stomp?

Sore Feet

I think some people don't do "The Devil Stomp" because they have sore feet. In Second Chronicles 16, King Asa took matters into his own hands and plotted against the people of God. He became an angry, manipulative king and the Bible records that he was diseased in his feet. What an analogy! When we become angry and manipulative, we lose our mobility and become powerless to move our feet. However, the Scripture says that in his sickness, Asa sought not the Lord. The sickness came because he didn't follow after God, and the sickness remained because he didn't seek God.

You can't do "The Devil Stomp" with disease in your feet. If you have been afflicted by the diseases of sin by your angry, conniving way, you may not be able to defeat satan. If you want to stomp the devil, you need healthy feet. The feet that carry good tidings are beautiful. Beautiful feet are obviously healthy feet. "...How beautiful are the feet of them that preach the gospel of peace, and bring glad tidings of good things!" (Rom. 10:15)

Have you lost your spiritual mobility? Are you getting sore feet? Maybe a corn or two? Spiritual calluses? God wants to heal your feet. God wants to give you the ability to "tread upon serpents" and be a devil stomper.

Foot Powder

If your feet have become sore, corned or calloused, you may need a sprinkle of foot powder. The Bible is full of stories and promises that make good foot powder. God cares about feet and provides for them. One of the greatest miracles God performed for the children of Israel when they were in the wilderness was to give them shoes that would not wear out. The Bible also says that their feet did not swell (see Deut. 8:4). God intends for His people to have good footwear. We must be prepared to move, to march, and to menace the enemy.

The Bible has much to say about feet. Following are some "footnotes" of mine:

- The ungodly image in Daniel was hit and destroyed by a stone made out of the mountain. It was hit in the feet. I guess you could say it was "de-feeted." (See Daniel 2.)

- Jesus said to Peter, "I must wash your feet." It was symbolic of getting rid of the dust from the road of life. Peter said, "Not so, Lord." But Jesus said, "Then you have no part with Me." Peter answered, "Not only my feet but my hands and head also." We need clean feet for the journey. (See John 13:6-10.)

- The priests in the Old Testament needed blood upon the big toe of the right foot. We need "sanctified feet." (See Exodus 29:20 and Leviticus 8:23; 14.)

- When the priests carrying the Ark of the Covenant put their feet into the water, the waters parted. The

Scriptures teach us that they took stones from the Jordan River out of the place "where the priests' feet stood firm." There will be stones of remembrance where the feet of God's men stand today. (See Joshua 4.)

- "The steps of a good man are ordered by the Lord...." (Ps. 37:23).

- For rough roads God promised Israel iron shoes. (See Deuteronomy 33:25.)

- God said he would make our feet like hinds' feet. These are mountain climbing feet. (See Psalm 18:33.)

- David prayed for his feet to be plucked out of the net. We need untangled feet because we can't devil stomp with tangled feet. (See Psalm 25:15.)

- David said, "Our feet will not be moved." In other words, we are stable or sure-footed. (See Psalm 66:9.)

- Christ told His disciples to "shake the dust off your feet" against those who won't receive them. (See Matthew 10:14.)

- Christ's feet were nailed to the cross. His feet were nailed to make our walk profitable.

- The woman with the alabaster box anointed the feet of Jesus. (See Luke 7:38.)

- Many references are made to those at the feet of Jesus. For example, Mary sat at His feet seeking the "better" part. (See Luke 10: 38-42.)

- Christ Jesus is going to put all things under His feet. (See 1 Corinthians 15: 25-27.)

- The vision in the Book of Revelation depicts the feet of Jesus as fine brass. His feet were like pillars of fire. (See Revelation 1:15; 2:18; 10:1.)

We must have our feet healed! What better place than at His feet? Then we need to get our feet shod for the road. After that, we simply move out and keep walking.

Right now is the time to get your boots out! Polish them up! Get the heels repaired and put some metal plates on them! Then put them on, rise to your feet and begin to move! Start dancing! Dance on the grave of the devil. Do "The Devil Stomp!" Stomp him out of your life! We are preparing for the victory. We are getting ready to make one more lap around without the devil on our heels. We will march into New Jerusalem and leave satan with the eternal headache from our feet! "And the God of peace shall bruise satan under your feet shortly. The grace of our Lord Jesus Christ be with you. Amen" (Rom. 16:20).

Epilogue

A Word of Encouragement and Prayer for the Wounded

I want to share a personal word of encouragement to any reader who may be still hurting or feeling hopeless. Not everyone reading this book will be in that condition, but even "boot stompers" can use this story because they may know someone who might not be stepping so high. This is a word of encouragement to those who have become impatient with their own progress. For those who want to fly again but have no wings, I share this testimony and offer my prayer for deliverance. I want to leave you with "a wing and a prayer."

Not long ago I suddenly began to find feathers everywhere. I would pick them up from the strangest places. It seemed each time I looked down there was a feather on the ground. What could all these feathers mean? I didn't recall seeing any naked birds flying around. So where did all these feathers come from?

Then I realized God was trying to tell me something. He talks to me like that sometimes. But I noticed I was finding only one feather at a time. Then it became clear to me that the reason I only found one feather at a time was because feathers are usually lost one at a time. They don't all fall out at once. So I was sure God was speaking to me. "You, too, have lost some feathers," He said.

Later I recalled standing on the shores of the Atlantic watching the gulls circle overhead. I wondered if I could attract them so I rattled the bag of potato chips I had taken to the big rock with me. Sure enough, they came. One, then two and then too many for me to count. Gulls were everywhere. They were brave little birds. They picked chips from my fingers as I held them in the air. Then I noticed that they were picking at my shoestrings. They all seemed to be fully clothed but those feathers I had seen in the crevices of the rock came from somewhere.

Then I noticed some birds were missing a few. Some of those feathers I picked up were soft and downy; others were large and stiff. They were unique. The feathers were all shapes and sizes, as they were lost during different stages of life—the soft ones from the very young and the stronger ones from the older birds. One thing I knew, these birds were losing feathers as they flew.

I had been waiting upon the Lord for the renewal of my strength but felt like an eagle with no feathers. I stood on the cliff and looked out over the vast land. I wanted to fly but could not find the strength to mount up. Where did my feathers go? Where had my strength gone? Little by little the understanding came to me. We lose a few feathers in each difficult situation we go through, but they do grow back. We don't lose them all at once. In a healthy bird, it is called the "molting" process. It is a necessary and ongoing process that makes the bird stronger and able to fly higher. Only a sick fowl would lose too many feathers at once and not be able to survive.

Being the inquisitive person I am, I spoke with a veterinarian about broken feathers. His insight was unique. He said a broken feather can cause blood loss. Most often, it is not fatal because the bleeding stops when the quill is removed. If the quill is not removed, however, there is the potential of hemorrhaging to death. We can draw a parallel to our lives from this story about birds and broken feathers. Too often, people have "broken feathers" that are not removed. These broken feathers consume all their strength. But the broken feathers must go. We may find that we want to keep them because they are a reminder of the damage we sustain as we fly through life. But God wants renewal and we cannot be renewed without releasing the old. God will remove the old, broken things of our heart to allow new growth and higher flight.

Again I wondered, *Where did all the feathers come from? What wind blew, or what scrimmage occurred with another bird?* Then my mind wondered, *Where do we lose our feathers in life?* Some of you may have lost one in a moment of disappointment with God. You may have lost one when you lost that baby. What about when your children turned their back on the God you taught them to love? Did you lose one when the college you wanted didn't accept you? How about when you wanted to get into the military and they turned you away? Did a feather drop out during that marital crisis or perhaps the death of a loved one? I don't know where you lost them, but one thing is for sure: If you live on this planet, you have experienced loss. The fact remains that God has a plan to replenish your strength.

The enemy intends that you never fly again. But God plans to help you mount up with eagles' wings. God doesn't want you in a home for disabled eagles. In Alaska, I saw beautiful eagles that could not fly. They sat on a post while our guide talked about what they could do if they were well, and how they would never again join other birds in flight. Satan thinks he can do that to you, but let me encourage you. "They that wait upon the Lord shall renew their strength; they shall mount up with wings as eagles" (Is. 40:31). It certainly is a healthy eagle God intends to make of you. Waiting on the Lord is key to mounting up with wings.

When will you get your new wings? When will the feathers grow back? They will grow back one feather at a time. They will be replaced, but maybe over a period of weeks, months, or even years. We don't lose things all at once, nor do we get things back all at once. We must realize that getting our wings back will happen one feather at a time.

They that wait upon the Lord shall renew their strength; they shall mount up with wings as eagles; they shall run, and not be weary; and they shall walk, and not faint (Isaiah 40:31).

My own testimony is that I fully recovered from the bout with depression I shared earlier in this book. I no longer stand staring into space wondering when I will fly. Today, I spread my wings and feel the wind of God surge underneath. Oh, the beauty and the splendor! Up here, I see the face of God...I can fly.

A Prayer for Your Victory

Lord, may your grace surround my friend
at this very moment, whoever he is.

Dear Jesus, rekindle his passion.
Put the spark back in his eyes;
fan the flame within him.

Lord, may your love sustain my friend
at this very moment, wherever he is.

Dear Jesus, restore his soul.
Put your Holy Spirit within him.
Make him completely whole.

Lord, may your power strengthen my friend
at this very moment, whatever his need.

Mary Martha Ministries International

Dianne Sloan, Founder/Director

1940 Millville Ave.
Hamilton, OH 45013
(513) 887-LIFE

www.DianneSloan.org

Email: DevilShrinker@aol.com

In His Word   At His Work

The Story Of Columbine

Excerpt from *The Martyrs' Torch:*
The Message of the Columbine Story

"I am not going to apologize for speaking the name of Jesus,
I am not going to justify my faith to them,
and I am not going to hide the light that God has put into
me. If I have to sacrifice everything... I will. I will take it."

Personal Journal Entry, Rachel Joy Scott, April 20, 1998

The blood of the martyrs is the seed of the church.

Tertullian

After her death, Rachel's family discovered her personal journals. They revealed a deep, secret relationship with Jesus that even her family knew little about. Rachel walked in a depth of relationship with Jesus that displayed a wisdom far beyond her years, and she actually seemed to foreshadow her death in several entries.

One of her personal journals was delayed in being returned to her family for several weeks after her death because it was in her backpack when she died. One of the bullets that passed through her small body was discovered inside her backpack and was considered police evidence until officially released. This bloodstained journal portion is breathtaking in ways you will soon discover.

Rachel surely loved her mother and father very much. Tragically, her family was all too typical of so many broken homes in our times. In her younger years, her dad was a pastor and her family a typical pastor's family. Sadly, in spite of such a nurturing, spiritual family structure, her mother and father tragically divorced more than ten years ago, when Rachel was a young child. After the divorce was final, Beth and Darrell had joint custody of the five children, Bethanee, Dana, Rachel, Craig, and Mike.

During those years Beth scrimped and saved, going to school at night while working during the day to support her children. Her son Craig once told me that he would sometimes hear her praying and crying in her bedroom late at night when times were especially hard.

A few days before Mother's Day, just weeks after Rachel's death, Beth was tenderly going through some of her daughter's many writings and drawings. From one of the stacks of papers, a page fell out into Beth's hands. There, in the beautiful script that only Rachel could write, and as a timely gift from a most loving heavenly Father, was the following poem:

SACRIFICE
should be her name,
because she has given up so much for us.

HUMBLE
should be her name,
because she will never admit the great things she has done.

FAITH
should be her name,
because she has enough to carry us, as well as herself,
through this crazy world.

STRENGTH
should be her name,
because she had enough to bear and take care of five children.

WISDOM
should be her name,
because her words and knowledge are worth more than gold.

BEAUTIFUL
should be her name,
because it is not only evident in her face,
but in her heart and soul as well.

GRACEFUL
should be her name,
because she carries herself as true woman of God.

LOVING
should be her name,
because of the deepness of each hug and kiss she gives us.

ELIZABETH
is her name,
but I call her giving, humble, faithful,
strong, wise, beautiful, graceful, loving mom.

What mother does not yearn to hear such words of tender devotion from her daughter? Rachel has been described by her family as possessing a certain impish joy and uninhibited zeal for life. She would wear funny hats and took joy in wearing clothes that set the pace for fashion as she saw it. Her sisters told me that Rachel once put a message on the family phone recorder that said, "Hello, this is Princess Rachel. Which of her loyal subjects would you like to speak with?" Never at a loss for words, Rachel would say what she thought or felt, and she had a certain refreshing transparency toward everyone. She possessed a highly creative music talent. Her friends spoke of how she would sit at the piano and play the most beautiful music, enrapturing her listeners. When they begged her to play it again, she'd giggle and say she couldn't remember it because she had just made it up!

Once, while performing the mime presentation of "Watch the Lamb" to the music of Ray Boltz to her schoolmates at Columbine, the music suddenly stopped right in the middle of the performace. Well, Rachel just kept dancing! She went faithfully through the motions of her performance while several of her schoolmates chuckled. At last, when the music finally came on again, she was perfectly in sync with it! Everyone was amazed and moved by Rachel's tenacious determination. She won the respect of her classmates that night.

What was ironic about this incident is the fact that the young man who ran the sound system that evening was none other than Dylan Klebold. The music stopped in Rachel's life once, but she kept dancing. The second and final time the music stopped was when Rachel was killed. She is still dancing! No evil or power on earth can stop the heavenly music to which Rachel Joy Scott dances now.

Rachel's journals clearly reveal that she believed her time on earth would be brief. Her writings show a young woman fervent in her desire to serve God. Following is the last known entry in her dairy.

"Am I the only one who sees?
Am I the only one who craves Your glory?
Am I the only one who longs to be forever in Your loving arms?
All I want is for someone to walk with me through
these halls of a tragedy.
Please give me a loving friend who will carry Your name in the end.
Someone who longs to be with You.
Someone who will stay forever true."

At the Columbine Torchgrab Youth Rally, held in Littleton on August 7, Rachel's 16-year-old brother, Craig, said of his sister:…

The Martyrs' Torch
ISBN 0-7864-2046-6

Available at your local Christian bookstore.

For more information and sample chapters, visit www.reapernet.com

Exciting title
by Os Hillman

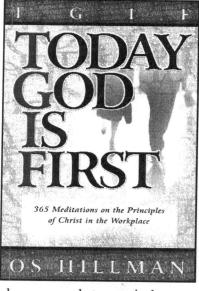

TODAY GOD IS FIRST

Yes, we all know that God is first every day, or at least He should be first. But can I be real for just a moment? Sometimes it is hard to keep Him first in my day. It is a struggle to see Him in the circumstances of my job. I need help to bring the reality of my Lord into my place of work.

Os Hillman has the uncanny ability to write just to my circumstance, exactly to my need. He helps me see from God's view. He strengthens my faith and courage to both see God and invite Him into the everyday trials and struggles of work.

So take this book to work, put it on your desk or table. Every day, just before you tackle the mountains before you, pause long enough to remind yourself—Today, God is First. Read the devotion, seal it with prayer and then go win the day for yourself, your Lord and your work.

Excerpt from February 14

The disciples were traveling across the lake to Capernaum when a strong wind arose and the waters grew rough. Suddenly they saw a figure on the water, and they were terrified until Jesus called out to them and identified Himself.

Isn't that the first thing we do when unexpected calamities or even something that we have never experienced before comes into our life? We panic until we can see that God is behind these events in our lives.

ISBN 0-7684-2049-0

Books to help you grow strong in Jesus

⟵ LADY IN WAITING
by Debby Jones and Jackie Kendall.
This is not just another book for single women! The authors, both well-known conference speakers, present an in-depth study on the biblical Ruth that reveals the characteristics every woman of God should develop. Learn how you can become a lady of faith, purity, contentment, patience—and much more—as you pursue a personal and intimate relationship with your Lord Jesus!
ISBN 1-56043-848-7
Devotional Journal and Study Guide
ISBN 1-56043-298-5

⟵ FROM THE FATHER'S HEART
by Charles Slagle.
This is a beautiful look at the true heart of your heavenly Father. Through these sensitive selections that include short love notes, letters, and prophetic words from God to His children, you will develop the kind of closeness and intimacy with the loving Father that you have always longed for. From words of encouragement and inspiration to words of gentle correction, each letter addresses times that we all experience. For those who diligently seek God, you will recognize Him in these pages.
ISBN 0-914903-82-9

⟵ AN INVITATION TO FRIENDSHIP: From the Father's Heart, Volume 2
by Charles Slagle.
Our God is a Father whose heart longs for His children to sit and talk with Him in fellowship and oneness. This second volume of intimate letters from the Father to you, His child, reveals His passion, dreams, and love for you. As you read them, you will find yourself drawn ever closer within the circle of His embrace. The touch of His presence will change your life forever!
ISBN 0-7684-2013-X

⟵ DON'T DIE IN THE WINTER...
by Dr. Millicent Thompson.
Why do we go through hard times? Why must we suffer pain? In *Don't Die in the Winter...* Dr. Thompson, a pastor, teacher, and conference speaker, explains the spiritual seasons and cycles that people experience. A spiritual winter is simply a season that tests our growth. We need to endure our winters, for in the plan of God, spring always follows winter!
ISBN 1-56043-558-5

⟵ UNDERSTANDING THE DREAMS YOU DREAM
by Ira Milligan.
Have you ever had a dream in which you think God was speaking to you? Here is a practical guide, from the Christian perspective, for understanding the symbolic language of dreams. Deliberately written without technical jargon, this book can be easily understood and used by everyone. Includes a complete dictionary of symbols.
ISBN 1-56043-284-5

Available at your local Christian bookstore.

Exciting titles
by T.D. Jakes

Destiny Image proudly introduces the T.D. Jakes Classics Gift Set

Includes #1 Best-seller, Woman, Thou Art Loosed, and Best-sellers, Can You Stand to Be Blessed, and Naked and Not Ashamed

With words that stand the test of time, T.D. Jakes' three books cross denominational lines, racial barriers, and gender biases to reach into the heart of the reader. With the compassion of Jesus Christ, he touches the hidden places of every woman's heart to bring healing to past wounds with the phenomenal best-selling *Woman, Thou Art Loosed!* With the same intensity he calls all men, women, and children to stop being afraid to reveal what God longs to heal in *Naked and Not Ashamed*. Only when we drop our masks and facades can we be real before our Lord and others. And with *Can You Stand to Be Blessed?* T.D. Jakes, a man of many accomplishments and life goals, shares personal insights that will help all people survive the peaks and valleys of daily living out God's call upon their lives. This classics gift set is sure to become a special part of every reader's personal library!
ISBN 1-56043-319-1 (Gift Set)

Also available separately.
WOMAN, THOU ART LOOSED!
ISBN 1-56043-100-8

CAN YOU STAND TO BE BLESSED?
ISBN 1-56043-801-0

NAKED AND NOT ASHAMED
ISBN 1-56043-835-5

Available at your local Christian bookstore.

For more information and sample chapters, visit www.reapernet.com

Exciting titles
by Myles Munroe

Exciting titles
by Michael L. Brown

▬ FROM HOLY LAUGHTER TO HOLY FIRE

America is on the edge of a national awakening—God is responding to the cries of His people! This stirring book passionately calls us to remove the roadblocks to revival. If you're looking for the "real thing" in God, this book is must-reading! (A revised edition of *High-Voltage Christianity*.)
ISBN 1-56043-181-4

▬ IT'S TIME TO ROCK THE BOAT

Here is a book whose time has come. It is a radical, noncompromising, no-excuse call to genuine Christian activism: intercessory prayer and the action that one must take as a result of that prayer.
ISBN 1-56043-106-7

▬ HOW SAVED ARE WE?

This volume clearly challenges us to question our born-again experience if we feel no call to personal sacrifice, separation from the world, and the hatred of sin. It will create in you the desire to live a life truly dedicated to God.
ISBN 1-56043-055-9

▬ OUR HANDS ARE STAINED WITH BLOOD

From the first "Christian" persecutions of the Jews in the fourth century to the horrors of the Holocaust, from Israel-bashing in today's press to anti-Semitism in today's pulpits, this shocking and painful book tells the tragic story that every Christian must hear.
ISBN 1-56043-068-0

▬ THE END OF THE AMERICAN GOSPEL ENTERPRISE

In this important and confrontational book, Dr. Brown identifies the sore spots of American Christianity and points out the prerequisites for revival.
ISBN 1-56043-002-8

▬ WHATEVER HAPPENED TO THE POWER OF GOD

Why are the seriously ill seldom healed? Why do people fall in the Spirit yet remain unchanged? Why can believers speak in tongues and wage spiritual warfare without impacting society? This book confronts you with its life-changing answers.
ISBN 1-56043-042-7

Available at your local Christian bookstore.